Divorce and Remarriage
A Primer for Christians

Divorce and Remarriage
A Primer for Christians

David L. Smith

WIPF and STOCK Publishers
Eugene, Oregon

DIVORCE AND REMARRIAGE: A PRIMER FOR CHRISTIANS

Copyright © 2008 David L. Smith. All rights reserved. Except for brief quotations in critical publications or reviews, no part of this book may be reproduced in any manner without prior written permission from the publisher. Write: Permissions, Wipf and Stock Publishers, 199 W. 8th Ave., Eugene, OR 97401.

ISBN 13: 978-1-55635-429-8

www.wipfandstock.com

Manufactured in the U.S.A.

To Gail
My beloved wife, friend, and soul-mate
For forty-three years

CONTENTS

Preface		1
Introduction		3
ONE	A History of Divorce and Remarriage	7
TWO	Divorce and Remarriage Today	21
THREE	Marriage in the Biblical Teaching	29
FOUR	Divorce and Remarriage in Biblical Teaching	39
FIVE	Moral Aspects of Divorce and Remarriage	71
SIX	Practical Implications	81
	Excursus: Clergy Divorce	93
	Select Name and Subject Index	99
	Index of Scriptures	107

PREFACE

This book is very near and dear to my heart. It comes out of my personal experience as a pastor in dealing with the subject of divorce, particularly in regard to the marriage of a single person to a divorced person or of two divorced persons.

As a young pastor, I found that the easiest way to deal with the divorce problem was to ignore it. When a couple came to me seeking marriage, I would ask, "Have you ever been married before?" If the answer from either was positive, I would refuse to marry them, usually telling them, "There's a pastor about three miles down the road. He will marry anybody!" Divorce was wrong; my mind was made up; don't attempt to confuse me with exceptions.

Then I was called to a larger church where several of the leading people were divorced and remarried. They were fine Christians, and it was obvious to me that God was using them in a wonderful way to achieve His Kingdom purposes. I began to realize that it was time for me to rethink my position and examine more closely what the Bible said about divorce and remarriage.

My search took me to the Southern Baptist Theological Seminary in Louisville, Kentucky, where I did a Ph.D. in New Testament Theology (with minor areas in Old Testament Theology, Old Testament Literature, and New Testament Interpretation). My dissertation topic was "A Theology of Divorce and Remarriage." God also led me during those years to pastor a small Southern Baptist church where many of the people had been divorced and remarried or who had married a divorced person. What a learning experience!

This book is based on the results of my dissertation research. But I have attempted to update the material and delete much of the academic language to make it more "user friendly." For those, however, who wish to delve into the material in a more scholarly fashion, there is considerable discussion of varying viewpoints contained in the notes with each chapter. In fact, the material is arranged so that individuals who wish to construct their own theology of divorce may work through it in a systematic manner and arrive at their own conclusions.

If this work proves helpful to pastors and lay people as they struggle with this painful problem, it will have achieved its purposes.

David L. Smith
Waterloo, Ontario
April 2008

Introduction

Few spiritual problems have caused greater perplexity in the Christian church than has divorce. The problem seems to be more pronounced now than in times past. What was an exception among practicing Christians half a century ago has now become commonplace.

For those who take the function of Scripture to be an all-sufficient guide in matters of faith and practice, the dissolution of marriage presents a serious dilemma. Most church members have interpreted the Bible as prohibiting divorce (except, perhaps, where adultery has occurred). Such an interpretation leaves Christian people in an agonizing situation. They are torn between what they think the Bible teaches and their own fears and feelings towards the divorced. This inner tension frequently causes an inability to relate or minister effectively to the divorced.

Nor is it much easier for the one who has undergone the trauma of divorce. Such a separation may be secondary only to the death of a spouse (in some ways it may be worse, for the finality of death is precluded by the continued presence of the former spouse in the community). The divorced person needs help and comfort, but the place to which one would normally turn for affirmation and council — the church — has too often become a place of estrangement. The divorced person is sometimes treated as a pariah by fellow-Christians.

Does the Bible teach that divorce (and subsequent remarriage) is sinful? Or is it permitted? If sinful, can it be forgiven? How should the Christian community treat one of its members who becomes divorced? What can the church do to strengthen marriage, inhibit divorce, and minister to the victims of marriage breakdown? These and other questions pertaining to the problem need straightforward answers from church leadership. And unless and until leaders give careful consideration to the biblical and theological implications of marriage and divorce, these much-needed answers will not be forthcoming. The church will continue to wallow in a slough of vacillation and fear in its treatment of this difficult issue and those embroiled in it.

For evangelical Christians, the Bible is the divinely-inspired and authoritative guide to Christian living. At the same time, we must recognize that believers live *by* the Bible and not *in* the Bible. They live, rather, in the context of a particular history and culture.[1] In matters of faith and practice, Scripture and the tradition of the Christian community are two sides of the same coin of spiritual truth, although when there is any discrepancy between the two, Scripture must be accorded supremacy.[2] Properly used, the tradition of the Christian community possesses an immense value as an instrument both to help interpret the Scriptures and, at the same time, to guard against the caprice of experience and the narrow interests of any particular age.[3]

This book begins, therefore, by reviewing the varied responses of the church throughout history to the issues of divorce and remarriage. It includes those groups which have contributed most to conservative thought: the early church, Roman Catholicism, the Continental Reformers, and the English churches. An overview of contemporary theological attitudes follows, sub-divided into Roman Catholic (both official and dissenting) and Protestant (including "broad" and "strict") viewpoints. It is hoped that these two chapters will serve to inhibit any radical or parochial interpretation, and that they will keep the entire matter in reasonable perspective.

Because one cannot do full justice to the divorce issue without first giving attention to marriage, the next chapter involves a study of the biblical and theological foundations of marriage and how these may relate to the problem at hand.

The discussion comes to a focus in chapters four, five, and six, which comprise a thorough investigation of the biblical teachings on divorce and possible remarriage. The various Old and New Testament passages are examined and the major ones are critically analyzed. The theological ramifications are set forth in chapter five, on the moral aspects of divorce and remarriage. These aspects include both those that are explicitly delineated and those that may be inferred from the Bible.

The conclusions are found in the sixth chapter, which deals with the implications of the preceding study for the church: those for the

---

1 George W. Peters, Introduction to Gene A. Getz, *Sharpening the Focus of the Church* (Chicago: Moody Press, 1974), 10.
2 Clark H. Pinnock, "How I Use Tradition in Doing Theology," *TSF Bulletin*, 6 (Sept.-Oct. 1982), 2.
3 David F. Wells, "The Role of Tradition for Pinnock and Dulles," *TSF Bulletin*, 6 (May-June 1983), 5.

Christian fellowship as a whole, for divorced persons themselves, and for the leadership of the church.

An excursus on the divorced minister follows. It examines the significance of divorce for continuing professional (especially, pastoral) ministry. Though not directly within the focus of the theme, it is nonetheless connected, and is of vital importance to the well-being of the church as a whole.

Chapter 1

A History of Divorce and Remarriage

The problem of divorce and remarriage is by no means a recent one for the church. From its inception, it has found this problem an irritant. Throughout the centuries, Christian leaders have grappled with the pros and cons of the matter.

The Attitudes of the Early Church

All peoples in the Roman Empire, regardless of their religious affiliation, had the right to divorce their spouses. Marriage was considered a private contract which, like all other contracts, might be dissolved. Divorce was easily attained and, because the state placed heavy financial burdens upon single people, remarriage was encouraged.[1]

One of the earliest writings (and a book regarded by many in the early church as almost on a par with the New Testament writings), *The Shepherd of Hermas* (c.140), deals with whether a husband sins if he continues to live with an adulterous wife. Hermas gives no option: he must divorce her. "At the same time, for the sake of her repentance," a second marriage was forbidden. Should an erring wife repent, her spouse must take her back in wedlock. Remarriage, other than to the repentant former wife, was regarded as adultery.[2]

In his *A Plea for the Christians* (c.177), Athenagoras showed that the typical resistance to remarriage was based on the church's understanding of Jesus' teaching on the matter. "Second marriage is only a specious adultery," he declared. "'For whosoever puts away his wife,' says He (meaning Jesus), 'and marries another, commits adultery.'"[3] Indeed, the marriage bond for many of the Ante-Nicene Fathers was so indissoluble that it continued beyond the grave. A virtually eternal relationship was established between the spouses, living or dead.[4]

---

1 Pat Edwin Harrell, *Divorce and Remarriage in the Early Church* (Austin, TX: R.B.Sweet, 1967), 173.
2 Hermas, *The Shepherd of Hermas*, Bk.II, Comm.IV:4–8, *The Apostolic Fathers, An American Translation*, ed. and trans. Edgar J. Goodspeed (New York: Harper and Row, 1950), 126.
3 Athenagoras, *A Plea for the Christians*, *The Ante-Nicene Fathers*, ed. Alexander Roberts and James Donaldson (New York: Chas. Scribner's Sons, 1908), 2.146–47.
4 J.P. Arendzen, "Ante-Nicene Interpretations of the Sayings on Divorce," *Journal of*

Tertullian (c.200), like his contemporaries, held that the marital bond is indissoluble. He strongly objected to a woman's remarrying even after her husband's death, because then she would have "one husband in the flesh and another in the spirit." This would be adultery, "joint knowledge of one woman by two men."[5] In regard to divorce, he claimed that the new law of Christ had abrogated the Old Testament law permitting divorce; that same new law thereby outlawed remarriage.[6] Tertullian did, however, accept remarriage if the dissolution of the first (either by death or divorce) had occurred prior to one's conversion (for in Christ, one becomes a new creation).[7]

Origen, in his *Commentary on Matthew*, did not seem as strict as his contemporaries. He noted that Christ rejected "the opinion that a wife was to be put away for every cause,"[8] but he did not seem to rule out divorce completely. Indeed, he admitted that some church leaders "have permitted a (divorced) woman to marry, even when her husband was living," and he confessed that such permission was "not altogether without reason," being undoubtedly a lesser of evils.[9]

The Council of Elvira (c.300) vigorously opposed remarriage. Women who divorced their husbands, regardless of grounds, were to be excommunicated. If an "innocent" wife (who divorced an adulterous husband) were to remarry, she was to be denied the sacraments until her first husband's death, after which she might find readmission to the church. Because, however, her crime was not as serious as that of a "guilty" party, if she were to die before her first husband, she might receive the sacrament of extreme unction.[10]

The Council of Arles (314) was more lenient in its outlook than the preceding Council. It dealt with the young Christian whose wife became an adulteress. Its counsel was similar to that of Elvira, that he should refrain from marrying a second time as long as the adulterous wife lived. No mention was made, however, of excommunication should he remarry.[11]

Theological Studies, 20 (1919), 233.
5 Tertullian, *Treatises on Marriage and Remarriage*, Ancient Christian Writers, trans. W.P. LeSaint, ed. Johannes Quasten and Joseph C. Plumpe (Westminster, MO: Newman Press, 1951), 13.93.
6 Tertullian, 103.
7 *Ibid.*, 96–97.
8 Origen, *Commentary on Matthew*, I.xiv.16, *The Ante-Nicene Fathers*, ed. Alan Menzies (New York: Chas. Scribner's Sons, 1908), 9.505.
9 *Ibid.*, I.xiv.23, 510.
10 Arendzen, 238–39.
11 Harrell, 182–83. Even though sometimes expressed in terms only of the male, there was nonetheless a concern for the female as well on the part of the Ante-Nicene Fathers.

Roman Catholic Attitudes

The teaching of the Roman Catholic Church was based on the formulations of Augustine of Hippo, who regarded marriage as a sacrament. His views were more clearly organized by Thomas Aquinas and were later incorporated into its Canon Law.[12]

The Fathers of the fourth and fifth centuries were very strict in their interpretation of the New Testament divorce sayings. Jerome (347-420), for example, believed that a wife might leave a husband who was guilty of sexual perversion; "yet he is still her husband and, so long as he lives, she may not marry another."[13] Should she divorce her husband and remarry, both she and the new spouse would be guilty of adultery. They could not receive the Eucharist (Lord's Supper) until they had done penance by agreeing to refrain from further sexual intercourse.[14]

For Augustine, "even from the union of the two, the man and woman, marriage bears a certain sacramental character, (which) can no way be dissolved by the death of one of them."[15] Such a sacramental bond holds in spite of adultery or divorce. Accordingly, he argued that, while divorce is permissible because of fornication on the part of one spouse (though he candidly admitted that he did not know whether fornication referred to "acts of uncleanness" or to "every transgression of the law on account of unlawful lust," (e.g. idolatry or covetousness), remarriage is out of the question for, regardless of circumstances or who may be the guilty party, the marriage bond remains.[16] Unless and until the original spouse dies, remarriage is adultery.

Thomas Aquinas' *Summa Theologica* set forth systematically what has become the teaching of the Roman Catholic Church on marriage and divorce. Marriage, he declared, "was instituted in the New Law in so far as it represents the mystery of Christ's union with the Church, and in this respect it is a sacrament of the New Law."[17]

---

12 Nolan Patrick Harrington, "The Historic Attitude of the Christian Churches Concerning Marriage, Divorce, and Remarriage," Diss. Southern Baptist Theological Seminary, 1948, 125.
13 Jerome, *Letters and Selected Works, A Select Library of the Nicene and Post-Nicene Fathers of the Christian Church*, ed. Philip Schaff and Henry Ware (New York: Christian Literature Co., 1893), 2nd ser., 6.110.
14 *Ibid.*, 111.
15 Augustine, *On the Good of Marriage*, I, *A Select Library of the Nicene and Post-Nicene Fathers of the Christian Church*, ed. Philip Schaff (Buffalo: Christian Literature Co., 1887), 1st ser., 3.406.
16 Augustine, *Our Lord's Sermon on the Mount*, Schaff, 6.18–19.
17 Thomas Aquinas, *Summa Theologica*, trans. English Dominican Fathers (New York: Benziger, 1948), 3.2716.

Nothing "not even adultery" can dissolve the marriage of two communicants. While a husband is bound to divorce a wife who continuously commits adultery, he may not remarry (to do so constitutes adultery on his part) unless she dies; should she repent, he should be reconciled to her, although he cannot be compelled to do so.[18] In the case where only one of the marriage partners is a believer, Aquinas taught that the unbeliever might be put away, because "spiritual adultery is more grievous than carnal."[19] At the same time, a distinction was made; should a communicant divorce an unbelieving wife who was willing to cohabit, he could not remarry; if the spouse, though, was unwilling, then "the believing husband after parting from her (might) be united to another in marriage."[20]

As products of the Renaissance, the Christian humanists attempted to cast off the tradition of the Church and return to the teaching of Scripture. Thomas More, for example, though he lived and died a Roman Catholic, and was even canonized by his church, nonetheless held views on marriage and divorce which were contrary to its tradition (he may have been motivated by having left a life of monkish asceticism to be married!). In his *Utopia*, he suggested that marriage is intended for the pleasure of male and female.[21] He stressed the importance of the marriage bond, but held that if a husband and wife could not live in harmony, by mutual consent of both they should be allowed to divorce and marry someone else.[22] He also believed that unfaithfulness or intolerable behaviour by either spouse breaks the marriage bond. At the same time, "breakers of wedlock are punished by the severest grade of slavery" in his Utopia and, for a subsequent offence, should be put to death.[23]

A colleague of More, Desiderius Erasmus also held views on marriage and divorce that were quite radical for his day. He cast scorn on the total prohibition of divorce and the idea of an indissoluble marriage bond.[24] Commenting on the Gospel of Matthew, he pointed out that the Church interprets Christ's teachings more narrowly than He did, and that such inflexibility is

---

18 *Ibid.*, 2794–98.
19 *Ibid.*, 2786.
20 *Ibid.*, 2787.
21 Valerian Paget, *More's Millenium, Being the Utopia of Sir Thomas More Rendered into Modern English* (New York: John McBride, 1909), 185.
22 *Ibid.*, 197.
23 *Ibid.*, 188.
24 Desiderius Erasmus, "Marriage," *The Colloquies of Erasmus*, trans. Craig R. Thompson (Chicago: Univ. of Chicago Press, 1965), 115–16.

contrary to the general interpretation of the Sermon on the Mount.[25] In treating the Pauline teaching on divorce, he noted a need to allow for remarriage after divorce for sound causes other than adultery, such as cruelty or mutual hatred. Erasmus maintained, though, that he was not seeking to encourage unnecessary divorces, but only to remedy unhappy marriages when all other means had failed.[26]

The twenty-fourth session of the Council of Trent in November of 1563 dealt with and set out the official Roman Catholic position on divorce and remarriage. In reaction against the Reformation, it reaffirmed the indissolubility of the marriage bond and the sacramental character of matrimony. It stipulated that "the bond of matrimony cannot be dissolved on account of the adultery of one of the married parties," and that neither spouse may contract a second marriage during the lifetime of another without committing adultery. If anyone should promote a contrary position, "let him be anathema."[27]

The decisions of the Council of Trent were further strengthened in 1880 by the issuance of *Arcanum Divinae Sapientiae* by Pope Leo XIII. It declared that "Christ the Lord raised matrimony to the dignity of a sacrament, and by the bond of divine love strengthened the naturally indissoluble partnership of a man and woman."[28] Moreover, Christ gave the Church complete control of marriage legislation. No civil authority has any legitimate right to regulate this realm.[29]

In 1930, Pope Pius X issued the encyclical *Casti Connubi*. Taking Leo XIII's encyclical as his starting point, he too emphasized the dignity of marriage as a perpetual sacrament.[30] Because marriage was instituted by God and affirmed by Christ, it is not subject to "human wills or to any contrary pact made even by the contracting parties themselves."[31] In regard to the indissoluble character of the marriage bond, the encyclical quoted Augustine of Hippo to the effect that there are no sufficient grounds. A woman's barrenness is not

---

25 V. Norskov Olsen, *The New Testament Logia on Divorce* (Tubingen: J.C.B. Mohr, 1971), 24.
26 Ibid., 26–27.
27 Theodore Alois Buckley, trans., *The Canons and Decrees of the Council of Trent*, 178, as quoted by Olsen, 39. While prohibiting remarriage after divorce, the Roman Catholic Church did (and still does) "annul" marriages for various reasons, permitting remarriage subsequent to the annulment.
28 Joseph Neuner and Heinrich Ross, *The Teaching of the Church*, ed. Karl Rahner (New York: Alba House, 1967), 359.
29 Ibid., 359.
30 Ibid., 361.
31 Ibid.

sufficient cause, nor is a husband's infidelity. If a separation occurs, any remarriage while a spouse lives is adultery.[32]

The Continental Reformers

The Protestant Reformation was essentially a reaction against what its proponents considered to be the ecclesiastical, moral, and theological deviations of Roman Catholicism. The Reformers sought to place the Christian faith back on a biblical foundation free of the trappings of magisterial dogma. Because of the varying origins of the Reformation, there is no one position on the ethics of divorce and remarriage. Nonetheless, one may find teachings that may be termed distinctively Protestant. These views are clearly seen in the teachings of Martin Luther and John Calvin, the most influential of the Reformation leaders. In general, they observed the Augustinian view that the good of the marriage involves children and faithfulness, but they rejected the sacramental view of the marriage bond, emphasizing the civil rather than the ecclesiastical aspects of matrimony.[33]

Martin Luther. Few have had a higher view of marriage than Luther. He taught that it has been established by God and that "marriage by nature is of such a kind that it drives, impels, and forces men to the most inward, highest spiritual state, to faith."[34] He decried attempts by the Roman Catholic hierarchy "to despise matrimony and to lure people away from it to celibacy." Few can remain chaste, and therefore, necessity dictates marriage.[35]

At the same time, while holding an exalted view of marriage, Luther did not consider it to be a church concern, but a worldly matter for the secular authority.[36] When Jesus spoke on divorce, said Luther, he was not legislating the issue, but preaching against a capricious use of the divorce laws.[37]

In his own preaching on divorce, Luther was quite flexible as to what constitutes just cause. He cited adultery as the only cause given by Jesus. Through the Mosaic Law, adultery was punishable by death. Therefore, an adulterer "has already been divorced, not by man but by God Himself, and separated not only from his wife but

---

32 Ibid., 363.
33 Roland Bainton, *What Christianity Says About Sex and Marriage* (New York: Association Press, 1957), 83.
34 Martin Luther, "Commentaries on I Corinthians 7," *Luther's Works*, ed. Hilton C. Oswald (St. Louis, MO: Concordia Press, 1973), 28.19.
35 Ibid., 26–27.
36 Luther, "On Marriage Matters," *Works*, 44.265.
37 Luther, "The Sermon on the Mount," *Works*, 21.93.

from this very life."³⁸ In such an instance, the other partner is completely free of any obligation to the former spouse. Adultery for Luther, however, was not the only possible ground. Desertion of spouse and family, he felt, was equally legitimate.³⁹

In his interpretation of the teachings of Paul, Luther believed that if a Christian hinders a believing spouse from following Christ, divorce is in order, with remarriage a viable option. On the other hand, should the Christian divorce the unbeliever for other causes, there must be reconciliation or the maintenance of a celibate state.⁴⁰ Anger was also a just cause. If a husband and wife could not live together harmoniously, but only in hatred and continual conflict, let them be divorced. Once more, however, reconciliation or celibacy was preferred. Nonetheless, in such cases, if a spouse did not desire reconciliation and the other was unable to remain chaste, the latter should remarry, for God does not require the impossible.⁴¹

John Calvin. Like Luther, Calvin held a high view of marriage, seeing it as "a good and holy ordinance from God."⁴² It was not, however, a sacrament any more than farming, building, or barbering, which were also ordinances, "for it is required that a sacrament be not only a work of God but an outward ceremony appointed by God to confirm a promise. Even children can discern that there is no such thing in marriage."⁴³ He scorned the Roman Catholic basis for sacramentalizing marriage by translating "mystery" in Ephesians 5:32 as "sacrament," concluding that Catholics were either deceived by the meaning of the Latin word or else ignorant of the Greek language.⁴⁴ At the same time, he insisted that marriage was instituted by God as a perpetual law in force until the end of the world.⁴⁵ Any rupture of that law has its origin in the depravity of humanity.

For believers, marriage is an indissoluble bond, and spouses connected by marriage no longer have the freedom to change their mind and go off elsewhere.⁴⁶ If they find it impossible to live with each other, they are bound nonetheless and may not take a new

---

38 Ibid., 96.
39 Ibid., 97.
40 Luther, "1 Cor. 7," 33–34.
41 Ibid., 32.
42 John Calvin, *Institutes of the Christian Religion, The Library of Christian Classics*, trans. Ford L. Battles, ed. John T. McNeill (Philadelphia: Westminster Press, 1950), 21.1481.
43 Ibid.
44 John Calvin, *Commentaries on the Epistles of Paul to the Galatians and Ephesians*, trans. Wm. Pringle (Grand Rapids: Eerdmans, 1955), 325.
45 John Calvin, *Commentary on a Harmony of the Evangelists, Matthew, Mark, and Luke*, trans. Wm. Pringle (Grand Rapids: Eerdmans, 1949), 2.381.
46 John Calvin, *Commentary on the Epistles of Paul the Apostle to the Corinthians*, trans.

spouse. On the other hand, if an unbeliever wishes to divorce a spouse on account of religion, the believer is no longer under marital obligation. In such a case, "the unbelieving party makes a divorce with God rather than with her partner."[47]

Like Luther, Calvin saw adultery as the one cause for divorce in Jesus' teachings. As far as he was concerned, the Old Testament penalty for adultery should be enforced, making divorce unnecessary, but "the wicked forbearance of magistrates makes it necessary for husbands to put away unchaste wives, because adulterers are not punished."[48] Divorce under such circumstances gives the innocent party freedom to remarry, for Jesus' condemnation of remarriage as adultery applied undoubtedly only to unlawful and thoughtless divorces.[49]

Although Calvin was very conservative in his theological view of divorce, like Luther his practice was more liberal. His "Ecclesiastical Ordinances," adopted by the Little and Large Councils of 1561, allowed three other grounds: impotence, extreme religious incompatibility, and abandonment. He also provided for annulment where a spouse could not, because of some physical infirmity, perform the conjugal act.[50]

British Church Attitudes

In the minds of the Continental Reformers, the insistence on the indissolubility of marriage regardless of circumstances was one of the foremost scandals of Roman Catholicism.[51] The British Reformers were equally critical of the Catholic position.

The early reformers. One of the early English reformers, and a martyr to his faith (d. 1536), was William Tyndale. His thought shows considerable Lutheran influence. Like the founder of the Reformation, he believed that marriage is ordained by God for purposes of love, companionship, and procreation, and to serve as a bastion against illicit sexual activity. It could not, however, be considered a sacrament in the proper sense of the word, for it did not carry with it a promise. Should it be considered such because it is a similitude of the union between Christ and his church, then all other New Testament counterparts would have to be considered

---

John Pringle (Grand Rapids: Eerdmans, 1948), 1.239.
47 Ibid., 244.
48 Ibid., 384.
49 Calvin, *Harmony*, 384.
50 John Calvin, "Ordonnances," *Corpus Reformatorum*, x.10–14, as cited by Olsen, 99.
51 A.D. Shepherd, *Marriage Was Made for Man* (London: Methuen, 1958), 67.

sacraments.⁵²

Much of Tyndale's consideration of divorce and remarriage was motivated by and applied to the divorce of King Henry VIII from Catherine of Aragon, and his subsequent marriage to Anne Boleyn. While not disallowing divorce when it accorded with scriptural grounds, Tyndale decided that the King's marriage to Catherine had been in full agreement with the Bible; he could find no good reason why the church should grant Henry a dissolution.⁵³

For Tyndale, divorce was possible only because of adultery. Because the Mosaic Law stipulated the death of the adulterer, the innocent party was not under bondage to the original marriage. Desertion was also a just cause in Tyndale's opinion, because he saw it as invariably tied to adultery.⁵⁴

Thomas Cranmer, first Archbishop of Canterbury following Henry's break with Rome (and martyred by Mary Tudor in 1556), played a key role in the formulation of Anglican views on divorce and remarriage. His attitudes reflected an affinity for Roman Catholic theology. He played a major part in the writing by a council of prelates of *The Institution of a Christian Man* in 1537, and was chairman of the commission which produced *A Necessary Doctrine and Erudition of Any Christian Man* in 1543, both of which were authorized by the King. Both books were similar in their emphasis that any marriage to which there was an impediment according to the laws of either church or realm must be declared null (and it was under this provision that Henry had his marriage to Catherine of Aragon declared null), but if a marriage was lawfully made according to the ordinance of God, it could not be dissolved during the lives of the spouses.⁵⁵

Cranmer's opinions are further evidenced in a letter in 1540 to Osiander, a preacher of Nuremburg (and his wife's uncle), where he derided the presence of Philip Melancthon at the second marriage of the Landgrave of Hesse. He was particularly dismayed at the idea of remarriage after divorce: "What can possibly be alleged in your excuse when you allow a man after a divorce, while both man and woman are living, to contract a fresh marriage?"⁵⁶

Martin Bucer, while in the strictest sense a Continental reformer,

---

52 William Tyndale, *The Obedience of a Christian Man* (Amsterdam: Theatrum Orbis Terrarum, 1977), fo. xc–xci.
53 S.L. Greenslade, *The Work of William Tindale* (Blackie and Son, 1938), 207.
54 Olsen, 112.
55 Arthur Robert Winnett, *Divorce and Remarriage in Anglicanism* (London: MacMillan, 1958), 307.
56 G.E. Duffield, ed. *The Works of Thomas Cranmer* (Philadelphia: Fortress Press, 1965), 307.

came to England in 1549 at the invitation of Archbishop Cranmer and spent the remainder of his life there. While in England, he wrote *De Regno Christi*, which strongly influenced many English divines. Much of the book was concerned with marriage and divorce.

Bucer emphasized the civil nature of marriage and reminded Edward VI (to whom the book was dedicated) that a monarch should see that marriages "be made, maintain'd, and not without just cause dissolved."[57] He castigated the Roman Church for its practice of disjoining persons from conjugal relations for reasons other than adultery while forbidding those so parted to remarry. Contrary to Roman Catholic interpretation of Scripture, he held that none of the Church Fathers ever dismissed a person from the church for remarrying after a divorce approved by Imperial law.[58]

For Bucer, the proper purpose of marriage was not sexual intercourse, but "the communicating of all duties both divine and humane, each to other with utmost benevolence and affection."[59] He concluded that marriage necessitates continuous cohabitation; if the marriage partners separate either mutually or against the will of the other, then the marriage is broken. In accordance with his view of the purpose of marriage, Bucer determined that not only adultery was just cause for divorce, but other separating factors as well, such as impotence, leprosy, and insanity.[60]

John Knox, the founder of Scottish Presbyterianism, was very much like his mentor, John Calvin, in his stance on divorce. In his *First Book of Discipline* (1560), he noted that marriage, once lawfully contracted, could not be terminated unless adultery had occurred. Like Calvin, he deplored the failure of civil authorities to execute adulterers. The church was to excommunicate such people and set the innocent party free to marry again. Upon the repentance of the guilty party, however, forgiveness was to be granted and, "if they cannot remain continent, we cannot forbid them to use the remedy ordained by God (i.e. marriage)."[61] Knox realized that such a position was far from perfect but, with his colleagues, he offered it "as the best counsel God giveth unto us in so doubtsome a case."[62]

The Dissenters. About one century after *De Regno Christi*, John

---

57 Martin Bucer, "The Judgment of Martin Bucer Concerning Divorce," *The Works of John Milton* (London: Wm. Pickering, 1851), 4.307. Milton translated these sections of *De Regno Christi* which dealt with divorce, placing them under the above title.
58 *Ibid.*, 313.
59 *Ibid.*, 329. His reasoning was based on Gen. 2:24.
60 *Ibid.*, 335.
61 William Croft Dickinson, ed. *John Knox's History of the Reformation in Scotland* (London: Thos. Nelson, 1949), 2.318.
62 *Ibid.*, 319.

Milton, one of England's greatest poets and a Puritan officer in Cromwell's Commonwealth government, not only translated Bucer's work, but also wrote two tracts of his own on the subject of divorce and remarriage: *Tetrachordon*, his major work, and *Colasterion*, both published in 1645 (Milton may have been motivated, in part, by his own unhappy marriage in 1643, which broke up shortly afterward, reunion being effected in 1645). According to its subtitle, the former was intended to harmonize the Old Testament passages on marriage and divorce (Gen.1:27f., 2:18, 23, 24; and Dt. 24:1f.) with similar passages in the New Testament (Mt. 5:31f.; 19:3–11; and 1 Cor. 7:10–16).

Milton inferred the grounds for divorce from the purposes of marriage as he had discovered them in the Bible. He noted that Genesis teaches that, because it is not good for man to be alone, God made a "help meet for him" (2:18, *AV*). Thus, the purpose of marriage is for companionship, mental and social as well as physical. Spouses, believed Milton, should help one another to be more devout, to generate mutual fellowship and love, to procreate, and lastly, to avoid sexual sin.[63] If a marriage is less than God intended, and is devoid of happiness, then it "is not of God's institution, and therefore no marriage."[64] Likewise, should a marriage be barren, though it might be very difficult for a man to divorce his wife, he would be justified in so doing. In commenting on Genesis 2:24, Milton agreed that a man should cleave to his wife, as long as she was what a wife should be. At the same time, he asked, "Can any law or command be so unreasonable as to make men cleave to calamity, to ruin, to perdition?"[65]

Milton had no problem reconciling his views with the Mosaic Law and Christ's interpretation of it. Jesus had no intention of abrogating Deuteronomy 24:1–4; He simply reproved its abuse.[66] He did not set out a new juridical law to be enforced by civil authority. Likewise, Paul, in his First Epistle to the Corinthians, was only imitating what Christ taught, that divorce is not to be hastily done, but that reconciliation should always be the first and foremost desire.[67]

Milton's views were not to go unchallenged. In 1647, the Westminster Confession of Faith was published. Its section on marriage stated categorically that nothing but adultery and wilful

---

63 John Milton, "Tetrachordon," *Works*, 4.158.
64 *Ibid.*, 157.
65 *Ibid.*, 166. Milton was not a "male chauvinist," for elsewhere, he notes that "the like may be said of a bad husband" (168).
66 John Milton, "The Doctrine and Discipline of Divorce," *Works*, 4.57.
67 Milton, "Tetrachordon," 247.

desertion is sufficient reason for dissolving the marriage bond.

John Wesley, the father of Methodism, demonstrated a break with the Reformers and a decided preference for the Anglican teaching out of which he came. He treated divorce and remarriage in the context of polygamy: "All polygamy is clearly forbidden in these words, wherein our Lord expressly declares, that for any woman who has a husband alive, to marry again is adultery."[68] The same held true for a man. Wesley did not allow divorce on the grounds of cruelty as did Luther and Calvin. The only ground was adultery, in which case there was no Scripture forbidding the innocent party from remarrying.[69]

The Divorce Bill of 1857. Prior to 1857, neither common law nor canon law made any provisions for divorce in England. Those wishing to have a divorce were obliged to secure a special Act of Parliament, a course open only to those with considerable financial means. In 1850, however, a Royal Commission recommended that marriage be made a civil concern and that a divorce court be established in which a husband might sue his wife for divorce on the ground of adultery. In this matter, the Commissioners believed that they were acting in accordance with the teaching of both the church and the Reformation.[70] A Divorce Bill was drawn up, but on its introduction, it met with such controversy that it was withdrawn and reintroduced with modifications several times. Finally, in June of 1857, it was passed and proclaimed as law.[71]

The Anglican bishops sitting in the House of Lords had been divided in their reaction to the Bill. The Anglican clergy was likewise divided, although a majority were deeply opposed to its passage. Among those protesting the Bill was Christopher Wordsworth, a Canon of Westminster (and, later, Bishop of Lincoln). He preached two sermons in the Abbey against the Bill: the first, "On Divorce," and the second, "On Marriage with a Person Divorced."[72]

In his first sermon, Wordsworth mentioned the desecration of marriage both by the establishment of civil marriage and by the creation of a court to grant divorces. He argued that the teachings of Jesus denied the right of divorce except for fornication. Such an allowance, however, did not mean that Christ affirmed that one

---

68 Edward H. Sugden, ed., *Wesley's Standard Sermons* (London: Epworth Press, 1921), 1.360.
69 *Ibid.*, 360.
70 David Atkinson, *To Have and to Hold* (London: Collins, 1979), 12.
71 Winnett, 135–42.
72 *Ibid.*, 148.

should put off one's spouse under such circumstances.[73] No more could be said than that He did not forbid it. Under no circumstances might a divorced woman remarry, even an innocent woman, for to do so constituted adultery.[74]

Wordsworth's second sermon reiterated the major points of the first, but dwelt on the theme of remarriage. He condemned the Divorce Bill as an encouragement to adultery and, by allowing remarriage, "it strengthens the cords of sin, and renders repentance very difficult. It could rivet two persons together in the bonds of iniquity..."[75]

Representative of those welcoming the legislation was F.D. Maurice in a sermon preached at Lincoln's Inn Chapel shortly after the Divorce Bill was proclaimed law. Maurice claimed that Jesus was not enacting new divorce legislation in the Sermon on the Mount. He was justifying Moses' legislation rather than condemning it. Moses was right in taking account of human frailty. As a result, Maurice welcomed the legislation and condemned the attitude of those opposed to it as a failure to discern the true nature of Jesus' teaching.[76]

To Summarize

The views of church leaders and scholars have been guided by their interpretation of the biblical teachings on marriage and divorce. Not all have interpreted these passages in like manner. Indeed, some have come virtually to opposite conclusions. Because they were writing largely for men, most of their remarks and illustrations concern women at fault. Generally, however, either directly or by allusion, they agree that what applies to one sex applies equally to the other.

The Ante-Nicene Fathers generally permitted divorce on the ground of adultery. Some even required it. At the same time, remarriage was usually forbidden. Not only did it cut off any chance of marital reconciliation, but many in the church regarded marriage as an indissoluble bond which continued unbroken until the death of one spouse. Thus (prior to such an occurrence), remarriage was an adulterous act and the offender was liable to excommunication. There was not, however, unanimity. Some, like Origen, allowed remarriage after a divorce on the ground of adultery. Others (e.g. the

---

73 Christopher Wordsworth, *Occasional Sermons*, ser.V, 203–04, as quoted by Winnett, 148–49.
74 Winnett, 149.
75 *Ibid.*, 151.
76 *Ibid.*, 151–52.

Council of Arles), while deploring remarriage, did not require excommunication as a penalty.

The Nicene and Post-Nicene Fathers were stricter in their interpretations of Jesus' sayings. No matter what a spouse had done, remarriage following divorce was out of the question. Augustine's position became the foundation of the Roman Catholic view of marriage as a sacrament. When contracted between two communicants, marriage is indissoluble. Where only one is a believer, spiritual adultery is involved and a divorce may be permitted (along with remarriage, under certain conditions). This position was challenged during the Renaissance by some of the Humanists (e.g. More and Erasmus), but it was reaffirmed during the Counter-Reformation by the Council of Trent as official dogma. Numerous impediments to marriage were noted, however, whereby marriages might be annulled.

The Protestant Reformation brought a fresh examination of the biblical teachings. The Continental Reformers, while holding a high view of marriage, eschewed its sacramental nature. They permitted remarriage by an innocent party after a divorce because of adultery or desertion.

The Anglicans generally held positions close to those of Roman Catholicism. While scandalized by the motion of marriage as a sacrament, they nonetheless tended to regard remarriage after divorce as adultery (although there were those who diverged from that opinion).

The dissenting denominations tended to follow the views of the Reformers. Some, like Milton, were very flexible as to cause, but most followed the Westminster divines in pronounced restraint.

Chapter Two

Divorce and Remarriage Today

Because of the varied views on divorce and remarriage assumed throughout history by the different factions of Christianity, it should not be surprising to find the full range of these opinions reflected among church leaders and scholars today. What is noteworthy, however, is the lack of agreement among theologians of the same denomination. Even in those groups where a magisterial dogma is set forth, there is dissent from the official position. Our purpose in this chapter is to survey the attitudes present among those of both Roman Catholic and Protestant persuasion in regard to divorce and remarriage.

Roman Catholicism

The Roman Catholic Church has always maintained the doctrine of absolute indissolubility vis-à-vis the consummated marriage of two communicants. In some cases it has held that, even on the ground of adultery, divorce with remarriage constitutes adultery.

The official view. The official Roman Catholic position has little changed since the "Canons on the Sacrament of Matrimony" were drawn up by the twenty-fourth session of the General Council of Trent in 1563. Marriage is a sacrament if both of those being united have been baptized according to the trinitarian formula (i.e. in the name of the Father, Son, and Holy Spirit). Because of its sacramental character, it is a bond which can never be broken. Thus, while separation of bed and board are possible, divorce is not.[1]

Certain marriages may, however, be terminated. An unconsummated marriage may be dissolved by papal dispensation or by one's spouse taking religious vows.[2] Marriages which come under the so-called "Pauline privilege" (i.e. where one partner is not a baptized Christian) may also be annulled. The local bishop reviews all divorce cases in his diocese and pronounces them either divorces or defective marriages. The former are regarded as infractions of canon law; the latter may be annulled.[3]

---

1 Bernard L. Ramm, *The Right, the Good, and the Happy* (Waco, TX: Word Books, 1971), 85.
2 A.R. Winnett, *The Church and Divorce* (London: Mowbray, 1968), 63.
3 Ramm, 85.

Because of the severity of the Roman Catholic canon law, it was hoped by many that the convening of Vatican II might bring some measure of relief, for its purpose was the modernization of Roman Catholic doctrine and practice. These hopes were dashed when the Council reaffirmed that the marriage bond is indissoluble and "will never be profaned by adultery or divorce."[4]

Nor were changes forthcoming at the Bishop's Synod on the Christian Family, held in the fall of 1980. Dermot Ryan, Archbishop of Dublin, spoke for the majority: "In expressing sympathy with those who experience difficulty in their married life, the synod cannot substitute compassion for moral principles."[5] Pope Paul VI closed the synod by continuing to refuse divorced and remarried Catholics participation in the Eucharist.[6]

Dissenting views. Not all of the Roman Catholic hierarchy or theologians are comfortable with the status quo. Many have challenged the magisterium, calling publicly for a more biblical and compassionate attitude in the Church's treatment of divorced and remarried persons.

During Vatican II, several bishops called for changes to the canon law. Archbishop Elias Zoghby, Patriarchal Vicar of the Melchites in Egypt, asked the Council to recognize the legitimacy of divorce on the ground of adultery, and to permit the remarriage of the innocent party. Lifelong continence resulting from separation would place an onerous burden on many.[7] Bishop Francis Simon of Indore expressed similar sentiments: "Laws, even the natural law, are for men, not men for the laws."[8]

In 1967, Victor J. Pospishil, an American priest of the Byzantine rite, called for fresh thinking on the doctrine of marriage. The church, he declared, must concern itself with the practical, rather than the ideal, condition of man in the world. It should realize that the God who so loved the world that he gave his only Son did not want to place an unbearable burden on people which would prohibit remarriage, "of course, within certain limitations."[9] The Church, he maintained, has divine authority to loose marriages as well as to bind them. Let it, therefore, have compassion on those who marriages

---

4 Walter M. Abbott, ed., *The Documents of Vatican II*, trans. Joseph Gallagher (New York: Guild Press, 1966), 253.
5 Francis X. Murphy, "Of Sex and the Catholic Church," *Atlantic Monthly*, 247 (February 1981), 52.
6 *Ibid.*, 66.
7 Winnett, 64.
8 *Ibid.*
9 Victor J. Pospishil, *Divorce and Remarriage: Towards a New Catholic Teachings* (New York: Herder and Herder, 1962), 127.

have failed. As it looses marriages, argued Pospishil, it will be God and not man who cuts asunder what he has joined together.[10]

Jack Dominian, a Catholic marriage counsellor, also called for a re-examination of canon law. He based his arguments on psychological concepts, concluding that consummation is not the criterion of marriage so much as love. Marriages where one spouse is psychologically incapable of love should be dissolved.[11]

James R. Hertel, a Jesuit, argued the case for a revision of canon law on both biblical and theological grounds. The Church has "institutionalized what in a real life situation can only be personalized."[12] Furthermore, by denying the right to divorce, it denies human beings freedom of choice and thereby precludes their coming before God as responsible agents. Thus, it fails to realize that marriage can be a sacrament only as long as there is human freedom of expression in the matter, which freedom the canon law has chosen to limit.[13]

Protestantism

Because of its historical insistence on the right of the believer to interpret Scripture for himself, Protestantism manifests a number of different views on divorce and remarriage, ranging from emphasis on the indissolubility of marriage to an acceptance of divorce and remarriage for virtually any reason whatsoever. Even in those denominations with a hierarchical structure (i.e. episcopal or presbyterian) which have set forth "official" positions on the matter, there is not unanimity. At the same time, it is possible to group most Protestant positions under two general headings suggested by Bernard Ramm: the strict Protestant view and the broad Protestant principle.[14]

"Strict" Protestantism. Historically, most Protestant clergy and theologians have held a high view of marriage and a very restrictive view of divorce. They typically fall into two categories, the first represented by Roman Catholicism and the second by John Calvin.

Most Protestants see marriage as a lifelong union, breakable only by death. While divorce may be permitted on the ground of adultery,[15] remarriage (other than to the original partner) is out of the

---

10 *Ibid.*, 127ff.
11 Jack Dominian, "Vatican II and Marriage," *Clergy Review*, 52 (1967), 31.
12 James R. Hertel, "Save the Bond? or Save the Person?" *America*, 11 (February 17, 1968), 218.
13 *Ibid.*
14 Ramm, 86.
15 There are those theologians who would refuse even this ground (see, above).

question during the lifetime of the former spouse. Any remarriage would be adulterous and both partners in such a new union would be subject to church discipline.

The Christian and Missionary Alliance is one denomination which holds an absolutist view. While in theory they allow for divorce on "positive scriptural grounds," according to the *Manual of the Christian and Missionary Alliance in Canada (2002)*, "a person is not to divorce his mate except for the cause of fornication."[16] No other causes are permitted. In the United States, persons divorced biblically *may* be permitted licensure for ministry.[17]

Baptist groups of a very conservative doctrinal stance (e.g. Bible Baptist Fellowship and independent Baptist groups) and conservative Pentecostal groups (e.g. Pentecostal Assemblies of Canada) hold similar views. They admit that the Bible does allow for divorce on the ground of adultery, but their pastors and polity generally prohibit the remarriage of a divorced person while the former spouse is living.

Many theologians of varying Protestant groups hold similar views. Charles Ryrie says flatly that "our Lord's teaching on divorce did not allow for it under any circumstances."[18] In the case of mixed marriages, Ryrie's stand on the "Pauline privilege" goes beyond Catholicism: divorce is permissible, but not remarriage.[19] Geoffrey Bromiley concurs: "a married person commits adultery (though divorced) if he or she lives with another while the first partner is still alive."[20] Gordon Wenham is equally adamant: "our Lord did not want his disciples to remarry after divorce… By declining to marry them in the church, we express our faithfulness to Christ's ideals."[21]

While not an inconsiderable number of Protestants hold the Roman Catholic view, a much greater proportion have adopted the Calvinist position, that Matthew 19:9 (and 5:32) and 1Corinthians 7:15 both allow for divorce under certain circumstances, with the right to remarry. Lutherans generally subscribe to this stance, stating that while marriage is taught as an indissoluble union and divorce is generally forbidden, the Bible does see in certain New Testament

---

16 "Statements: Marriage–Divorce–Remarriage," *Manual of the Christian and Missionary Alliance in Canada (2002)*, 79, as viewed on website www.cmacan.org/resourcespg.php?pg_id=157, July 2004.
17 See www.cmalliance.org/ncmserve/general.jsp, July 2004.
18 Charles C. Ryrie, *The Role of Women in the Church* (Chicago: Moody Press, 1970), 48.
19 *Ibid.*, 65.
20 Geoffrey W. Bromiley, *God and Marriage* (Grand Rapids: Eerdmans, 1980), 64.
21 Gordon Wenham, "May Divorced Christians Remarry?" *Churchman*, 95 (1981), 60.

passages the possibility for divorce and remarriage.[22]

The Church of the Nazarene, traditionally very unyielding in its view of divorce, has in recent years modified its stance from the Roman Catholic position to near Calvinism. Its 1976 *Manual* declares:

> Though there may exist other causes and conditions as may justify a divorce under civil law, only adultery is a scriptural ground for divorce and only adultery will supply such a ground as may justify the innocent party in remarrying...[23]

Nazarenes do not admit as just and proper the exception mentioned by Paul in 1 Corinthians 7:15.

Because of their insistence on local church autonomy, the mainline Baptist denominations (American Baptist Churches, Canadian Baptist Ministries, Southern Baptist Convention, etc.) hold no official position on divorce and remarriage. Their pastors, however, generally recognize the New Testament exceptions and remarry only those persons who meet that standard. There are, however, those who would better be included in the category of "broad" Protestantism, below.

Numerous theologians maintain the right to divorce and remarriage on the grounds of the exceptions of Matthew and 1Corinthians. Representative of such a view is John Stott, who teaches that, "while marriage is a permanent and exclusive union,... divorce (and therefore remarriage) is permissible on two grounds..."[24] These grounds are immorality and desertion.[25] Robert Stein agrees, holding that marriage is a lifelong union according to Jesus' teachings, although Matthew, inspired by the Holy Spirit, allows for divorce in the case of adultery. "It is not mandatory, but it is permissible."[26] He further cites Paul as permitting divorce in the case of the desertion of a Christian by an unbelieving spouse.[27]

"Broad" Protestantism. The broad Protestant principle suggests that the Bible does not give sufficient treatment on the subject of divorce and remarriage. While it provides some guidance, to any consideration of the matter must be added facts from medicine, psychology, and sociology. Without these additional factors, one cannot arrive at a satisfactory ethic for contemporary society.

---

22 James G. Emerson, *Divorce, the Church, and Remarriage* (Philadelphia: Westminster Press, 1961), 121–22.
23 *Church of the Nazarene Manual, 1976* (Kansas City, MO: Nazarene Publishing House, 1976), 47.
24 John R.W. Stott, *Divorce* (Downer's Grove, IL: Inter-Varsity Press, 1973), 27.
25 *Ibid.*, 28.
26 Robert H. Stein, "Is It Lawful for a Man to Divorce His Wife?" *Journal of the Evangelical Theological Society*, 22 (June 1979), 119.
27 *Ibid.*, 120.

The Eastern Orthodox churches must be placed almost on a middle ground between the strict and broad principles in divorce, but tilting towards the broad ethic. They permit remarriage following divorce on the ground of adultery. But this cause is viewed only as a point of departure for other similar grounds injurious to marriage, such as abortion, attempted murder, etc.[28]

Some churches have moved from a strict ethic to a broad one. The Anglican Communion is one of these. Most of its churches have followed the lead of the Anglican Church of Canada which, in 1967, passed a canon permitting the remarriage of divorced persons in the church, even though the former partner might still be living (a complete reversal of former policy). Permission to remarry depends upon any prior marriage having been validly dissolved, on an attempt by the applicant at reconciliation, and upon an assurance of stability for the prospective marriage.[29]

Many Presbyterian churches take quite a liberal view of divorce and remarriage. When, in 1958, a merger took place between the United Presbyterian Church of North America and the Presbyterian Church in the United States of America, a revised Westminster Confession was made to read that "remarriage after a divorce granted on grounds explicitly stated in Scripture or implied in the gospel of Christ may be sanctioned…"[30] To allow such grounds as explicit or implicit in the Bible is to allow for virtually unlimited cause.

The United Methodist Church has also accepted the broad principle. The 1956 *Book of Discipline* permitted marriage only for the innocent party on the basis of adultery, mental or physical cruelty. The latest (2000) *Book of Discipline* is much more lenient, making allowance for almost any cause, including estrangement that cannot be reconciled.[31]

The United Church of Canada, an amalgam of Presbyterians, Methodists, and Congregationalists, has gone to about as broad an ethic as any church could have. For some years, like the United Methodists, it has supported a very open policy on divorce. In 1988,

---

28 Theodore Mackin, *Divorce and Remarriage* (New York: Paulist Press, 1984), 373.
29 Anglican Church of Canada, "Canon XXVII: On Marriage in the Church," Part IV, Art. 2, Appendix to *Marriage, Divorce and the Church: The Report of the Commission on the Christian Doctrine of Marriage* (London: SPCK, 1972), 162–63.
30 *The Constitution of the United Presbyterian Church in the United States. Part One, Book of Confessions* (Philadelphia: Office of the General Assembly of the U.P.C.U.S.A., 1967), Art. 6.125.
31 "Divorce," *The Book of Discipline of the United Methodist Church* (Nashville: United Methodist Publishing, 2000), on website www.umc.org/interior.asp?mid=1723, July 2004.

its Division of Ministry and its Division of Mission went so far as to recommend to the church's General Council a completely open sexual orientation both of lifestyles and ministry which would prohibit any consideration of one's marital status or sexual orientation as germane even to ordination.[32]

As always, individual theologians seem to be on the cutting edge of the advance towards a more lenient divorce ethic. Emil Brunner, a twentieth-century pioneer of the broad principle, admits that, while the idea of indissolubility may be inherent in the idea of marriage, when love and fidelity have fled, "the only moral thing to do is to dissolve (the) marriage..."[33] Otto Piper takes an equally compassionate stance, declaring that divorce is a consistent termination of a marriage relationship where the partners are unable to mend the pieces together. It is true that Jesus did not legitimize divorce, but there may be obstacles to the continuance of a marriage with which couples just cannot cope.[34] Ramm condemns those churches which try to deal with divorce and remarriage in legalistic ways which deny love and compassion. Indeed, he warns, "to maintain a destructive marriage on the basis of being loyal to the

---

32 So, "Toward a Christian Understanding of Sexual Orientation Lifestyles and Ministry," Report, The United Church of Canada, February 19, 1988.
33 Emil Brunner, *The Divine Imperative*, trans. Olive Wyon (Philadelphia: Westminster Press, 1947), 361.
34 Otto A. Piper, *Christian Ethics* (London: Thos. Nelson and Sons, 1970), 303.

Christian ethic of no divorce is hardly justifiable."[35]

Summary

Roman Catholicism considers marriage to be an indissoluble sacrament if both participants have been baptized in the trinitarian name and have been united by a priest. Divorce is not permitted for any cause whatever, although separation of bed and board is. Some marriages, however, may be declared "defective" (e.g. the so-called "Pauline privilege" of 1Cor. 7:15, where one spouse has not been baptized), and may be annulled. Although many Roman Catholic theologians have challenged this position on biblical, theological, and humanitarian grounds, the Roman Church has remained unmoved.

Some Protestant denominations and theologians, while denying the sacramental nature of marriage, hold a view essentially similar to that of Rome. Some reject divorce and remarriage completely because they see marriage as an unbreakable, lifelong relationship. Others admit divorce for adultery (and, in some cases, for desertion), but forbid remarriage as long as the other partner lives.

More Protestants hold to a strict view of divorce and remarriage which allows, nonetheless, for the biblical exceptions. Some permit divorce with remarriage on the ground of adultery only. Others would include desertion or the insistence of an unbelieving partner on divorce.

The tendency of Protestantism, however, seems to be moving towards a broader ethic. It holds that, since New Testament times, factors have entered the matrimonial picture which Jesus could not have anticipated.[36] The church must attempt to develop a total ethic which takes into account these other psychological and sociological factors, and so can minister effectively in all possible situations. A larger ethic is needed than that which prevails in Scripture.

---

35 Ramm, 88.
36 The advent of the whole world as a small community (because of modern technology), increasing religious pluralism, and the abundance of working wives and mothers, are only a few of these factors which have so deeply influenced marriage and the home.

Chapter 3

Marriage in the Biblical Teaching

One cannot construct an effective theology of divorce and remarriage without first investigating the biblical concept of marriage. One's understanding and experience of what God intended marriage to be will determine one's view of divorce and remarriage. This chapter, therefore, will examine a number of significant biblical passages concerning marriage, and will set forth the theological implications which stem from the apparent nature and purpose of marriage in the mind of God.

The Old Testament Teaching

What the Old Testament has to say is fundamental to any Christian theology. It served as the Scriptures for the New Testament church, and the teachings of Jesus and his apostles are replete with references to and quotations from its writings.

Genesis 1:26–28. In the first chapter of Genesis, one finds the first record of the beginnings of male-female relationships. The creative work of God is brought to its apex with his decision to "create man in our image, corresponding to our likeness" (v.26). As to what the divine image may be is not clear. It has been argued that the original concept was corporeal, and was later spiritualized.[1] It has been suggested that the term means a "reflection," in that man, with his powers of natural transcendence and self-governing will, and man alone reflects God at the creaturely level as a free and responsible agent.[2]

The Hebrew word *adham*, translated in verse 26 as "man," must be seen, because of its context, to include both male and female. Both are made in the image of God; they stand equal in his sight. Both receive his blessing (v.28). It is evident here that God created man and woman to live in community with each other. Someone has observed that "the male is not even called man until he is united with the female,"[3] and aptly notes that the image of God in humanity is the

---

1 U. Cassuto, *A Commentary on the Book of Genesis*, trans. Israel Abrahams (Jerusalem: Magnes Press, 1961), 1.56.
2 Paul Jewett, *Man as Male and Female* (Grand Rapids: Eerdmans, 1975), 20.
3 Diana R. Garland, "'Male and Female He Created Them': Theological Perspectives on the Relationship Between Male and Female," Research Paper:

fellowship between man and woman.[4]

Genesis 2:18–24. The second chapter of Genesis is a complementary account of the creation of mankind.[5] The chief concern of verses 18–24 is the relationship between man and woman. It portrays God's remedy for human loneliness. Man was created as a social being. The words, "It is not good for man to be alone"(v.18), are illustrative of his greatest need. When God brought the animals and birds to man that he might name them, man's loneliness was all the more deeply emphasized. Every other creature had a counterpart, "but for man there was found no suitable helper" (v.20).

The account states (vv.21–22) that woman was fashioned from man's side. Had it not been so, declares one notable theologian, the "pre-eminence and unity of the human race in general would have been forfeited."[6] With the creation of the female, the man was able to fulfil his destiny as a social being.[7]

In verse 23, the writer emphasizes God's special role in the coming together of male and female by saying that He "brought her to the man." God is pictured here as the father of the bride, leading the woman to her mate.[8] The man's exclamation that the female is "bone of my bones and flesh of my flesh" demonstrates his recognition of their common origin as well as his joy in receiving one who corresponds so completely to himself. His comment is an excellent lead into the writer's interpretation of the passage as a description of the first marriage and as a model for all marriage (v.24). An instinctive urge for fellowship draws a man away from his parents to join himself to his wife, and the two become one. Nor is the union only physical. It is to be a spiritual unity, a vital connection of heart as well as of body.[9]

Southern Baptist Theological Seminary, 1983, 18. Cf. Diana S. Richmond Garland and David E. Garland, *Beyond Companionship, Christians in Marriage* (Philadelphia: Westminster Press, 1986), 24–30.
4 *Ibid.*
5 While there are some who would insist that ch.1 and ch.2 are different (some might even say, contrary) accounts of creation, the former from the Priestly redactor and the latter from the Yahwist, one must remember that it is the canonical or "final" form of the text which is authoritative, and not some scholar's reconstruction of the "original" form.
6 Franz Delitzsch, *A New Commentary on Genesis*, trans. Sophie Taylor (Edinburgh: T. and T. Clark, 1888), 1.143.
7 W. Gunther Plaut, *The Torah: A Modern Commentary* (New York: Union of American Hebrew Congregations, 1981), 31.
8 Gerhard von Rad, *Deuteronomy, The Old Testament Library* (Philadelphia: Westminster Press, 1966), 82.
9 C.F. Keil and Franz Delitzsch, *Biblical Commentary on the Old Testament*, trans. James Martin (Grand Rapids: Eerdmans, 1949), 1.90. Cf. Charles Nichols, "Some

Proverbs 5:15–19. Here, the monogamous male-female relationship is elevated as the ideal. The husband is exhorted to be united physically to his wife and to no one else. She is to be the entire source of his sensual pleasure (v.16).[10] He is urged to remain faithful to her and not to squander his virility elsewhere; in this way his children will truly be his and will not be strangers to him.[11] In verse 18, the same theme of fidelity is reiterated. Whether the hind and doe of verse 19 refer to the husband or wife is open to question,[12] but the thrust of the verse remains the same: the stress is on conjugal love. It is obvious, however, that continued physical excitement in a marriage of many years is possible only when love has deepened beyond mere sexual attraction.[13]

Malachi 2:14. The prophet condemns the Jew who dismisses his Hebrew wife to marry a woman from among the heathen (see 2:11).[14] He points out that, when the man married, "the Lord was a witness between you and the wife of your youth." Old Testament marriages were generally negotiated between families and the contract (either written or oral) was formalized by the payment of the *mohar*, or bride-price, to the bride's father.[15] While there seems to have been no formal religious rite accompanying the marriage, since Israel was a theocracy, it was held that God was a witness to the marriage agreement,[16] Thus, his wrath rested upon the one who was faithless to the marital agreement, for "she is your companion and the wife of

---

Musings on the Divorce Question," *Didaskalia*, 1 (November 1989), 18 who notes from this verse that "companionship is the primary purpose for marriage (even above procreation)." Cf. Craig Blomberg, "Marriage, Divorce, Remarriage, and Celibacy," *Trinity Journal*, 11 NS (Fall 1990), 166–67 for a fine summary of this passage, especially in regard to "oneness."

10 Crawford H. Toy, *A Critical and Exegetical Commentary on the Book of Proverbs*, The International Critical Commentary (Edinburgh: T. and T. Clark, 1899), 112.

11 W. Gunther Plaut, *Book of Proverbs, A Commentary* (New York: Union of American Hebrew Congregations, 1961), 77–78 points out that vv.16–17 have been taken by some Talmudic interpreters to mean that a man's faithfulness to his wife will not only ensure continued fertility in the marriage, but will also ensure his wife's fidelity.

12 With respect to opposing views, see Plaut, *Proverbs*, 78 and William McKane, *Proverbs, A New Approach*, Old Testament Library (Philadelphia: Westminster Press, 1970), 319.

13 Plaut, *Proverbs*, 78.

14 Possible motives may have been lust (the desire for a younger and more sensual woman) or security (power rested with the non-Jews); hence, it would have been advantageous both politically and economically to effect a heathen union.

15 E. Neufeld, *Ancient Hebrew Marriage Laws* (London: Longmans Green, 1944), 42–61.

16 Marcus Dods, *The Post-Exilian Prophets* (Edinburgh: T. and T. Clark, 1965), 144. There may have been other perspectives on marriage during this period, but only the prophetic views have been preserved.

your covenant." Marriage was a *berith Elohim,* or "covenant of God,"[17] and to repudiate one's lifelong companion (the Hebrew literally means "one bound to you") is a treacherous act.

The New Testament Teaching

The foundation of the Christian ethic of marriage is rooted in the Pentateuch. Indeed, much of the New Testament teaching is a reaffirmation of what one finds in the Old Testament, although the New Testament church often went beyond these teachings in adjusting to new situations and cultures.

Matthew 19:4–6.[18] While this passage is generally considered a "divorce passage," Jesus is actually affirming marriage. He refers to both Genesis 1:27 and 2:24, emphasizing the Jewish idea that creation is a model for marriage: "For this reason a man shall leave his father and mother, and shall be yoked to his wife; and the two shall become one flesh"(19:5). Just as God created one man and one woman and presented the one to the other, even so in marriage a single man and a single woman come together. The divine intention is that they become a unity. Therefore, one should not attempt to tear apart what God has united.

1 Corinthians 7:1–9. Paul's advice on marriage is given in the context of the licentiousness of Corinth. Evidently, the church there had written him inquiring about the appropriateness of sexual relationships, even in marriage. The Apostle replies that, while celibacy may be a laudable state,[19] not everyone can practice it. In an evil society, surrounded on every side by vice, marriage may be for some a necessary safeguard against falling prey to temptation (v.22).[20] The marriage relationship involves a reciprocity (v.30);[21] the husband does not belong to himself, nor the wife to herself. They belong to each other. Indeed, Paul warns against any prolonged abstinence from sexual relations unless it is by mutual consent for a

---

17 cf. Prov. 2:17, where the reverse occurs and the unfaithful woman forsakes the companion of her youth and the covenant of God.
18 Mark 10:6–9 is a parallel account and consequently is not examined. For a consideration of the Marcan version and a fuller treatment of Matthew, see chapter 4, below.
19 C.K. Barrett, *A Commentary on the First Epistle to the Corinthians* (New York: Harper and Row, 1968), 154 suggests that Paul in v.1 is quoting from their letter to him.
20 Archibald Robertson and Alfred Plummer, *Critical and Exegetical Commentary on the First Epistle of Saint Paul to the Corinthians, The International Critical Commentary* (New York: Chas. Scribner's Sons, 1911), 133 who also point out that v.2 is a prohibition of polygamy.
21 Hans Conzelmann, *I Corinthians, Hermeneia* (Philadelphia: Fortress Press, 1975), 117, n.24.

brief period, to allow more complete devotion to spiritual concerns. At the same time, he warns that a return to normal conjugal activity is imperative for, if sexual desire does not find a legitimate outlet, there is always a danger that Satan will tempt an unsatisfied spouse to fornication or adultery (v.5).[22] Paul does not make this abstinence a command, but allows it for those who favour asceticism (v.6).[23]

While affirming the married state, Paul does not want to detract from the importance of singleness. Considering the licence of Corinth, he might well wish for universal celibacy (v.7).[24] At the same time, he recognizes that celibacy is a gift from God to an individual. And so, he counsels the unmarried to remain single, if they are able (v.8). But, "if they do not have self-control, let them marry" (v.9).[25] It is, after all, better to marry and be able to exercise free sexual expression than to be burning continually with unsatisfied sexual desire.[26] If the gift of continence has not been received, then marry, for marriage is also a divine gift.

Ephesians 5:21–33. The writer's theme is mutual submission on the part of believers (v.21), and he shows how this submission is to be accomplished by husbands and wives. For wives, it involves showing deference to one's own husband (v.22). The phrase, "as to the Lord," does not mean that wives are obliged to give their husbands the same deference they would give to Christ, but rather that deference to their husbands is a part of their duty to the Lord.[27] For the husband, submission involves a sacrificial love for his wife (vv.28–29).[28]

Throughout the passage, the marital union is seen as analogous to the union of Christ and his church. Paul quotes Genesis 2:24 to demonstrate the unity of husband and wife in marriage, such

---

22 Barrett, 157.
23 Barrett, 157. But note, as well, contra this opinion, Conzelmann, 118, and Robertson and Plummer, 135–36.
24 Robertson and Plummer, 136.
25 Barrett, 161 reads this verse: "But if they are not living continently...," noting the implication that some members of the church were not succeeding in the celibate life and were succumbing to fornication.
26 For a good treatment of the significance of *purousthai* ("to burn") in this context, see Michael L. Barre, "To Marry or to Burn: *Purousthai* in I Cor. 7:9," *Catholic Biblical Quarterly*, 36 (1974), 193–202.
27 F.F. Bruce, *The Epistle to the Ephesians* (Old Tappan, NJ: Fleming H. Revell, 1961), 114. A good commentary on this verse is found in Col.3:18, where wives are to defer to their husbands "as is fitting in the Lord." Cf. Marcus Barth, *Ephesians 4–6, The Anchor Bible* (Garden City, NY: Doubleday, 1974), 610-11.
28 T.K. Abbott, *A Critical and Exegetical Commentary on the Epistles to the Ephesians and Colossians, The International Critical Commentary* (Edinburgh: T. and T. Clark, 1887), 171 points out that such love goes beyond simple ego-concern. It involves the affections whereby the man is as concerned for his wife's welfare as he would be for his own.

closeness being the ideal for all marriages, though few will realize it.[29] In fact, "the ideal of unity is seen only in the marriage of Christ and his Church, which itself sets a pattern for human marriage to emulate."[30]

Hebrews 13:4. This admonition on chastity and fidelity to the marriage vow follows an exhortation to brotherly love. It is set in a context where one might more readily take brotherly love for granted than sexual purity.[31] The writer emphasizes that God ordained marriage and will punish any intrusion upon its sanctity by a third party.[32] He makes a distinction between "fornication" (*moichoi*), married persons engaging in sexual intercourse with someone other than their spouse, and the "exceedingly perverse" (*pornoi*), married persons who engage in all sorts of illicit sexual perversions. The former term is referring mainly to the fracturing of another person's marriage vows; the latter, damage to one's own.[33] Neither will escape God's wrath.

The Theological Implications

From the biblical teachings, a number of theological implications may be derived.

Marriage as acceptance of God's invitation to participate in his creative activity. Marriage, according to the author of Genesis, goes back to before the Fall. It is based in the primeval relationship of male and female.[34] Man and woman were created for each other (Gen. 2:21–22) and saw a matching correspondence (Gen.2:23). Together they stood before God, participating in his image and likeness. It may be said, then, that marriage is an acceptance of God's invitation to participate in his creative activity.[35]

The woman completes the man's life by bringing to him a new, feminine dimension which he could not otherwise have. In turn, he gives her a masculine prospective which makes her a more whole

---

29 C. Leslie Mitton, *Ephesians, The New Century Bible Commentary* (London: Marshall, Morgan and Scott, 1976), 206.
30 *Ibid.* Cf. Barth, 74ff.
31 James Moffatt, *A Critical and Exegetical Commentary on the Epistle to the Hebrews, The International Critical Commentary* (New York: Chas. Scribner's Sons, 1924), 287. Cf. F.F. Bruce, *The Epistle to the Hebrews, The New International Commentary on the New Testament* (Grand Rapids: Eerdmans, 1964), who finds this verse a part of the exhortation on brotherly love.
32 Bruce, *Hebrews*, 392.
33 Moffatt, 227.
34 Helmut Thielicke, *Theological Ethics*, trans. John W. Doberstein (Grand Rapids: Eerdmans, 1964), 3.104.
35 Rudolf J. Ehrlich, "The Indissolubility of Marriage as a Theological Problem," *Scottish Journal of Theology*, 23 (1970), 296.

person than she could otherwise be.[36]

There are some who see the chief purpose of marriage as reproductive. But procreation is only one facet of the participation by an individual man and woman in God's creative work. Sex is an important gift from God, but the failure to reproduce does not negate the meaning of marriage. Sexual intercourse (within marriage) is itself significant. By this relationship the husband realizes more of what it is to be a man, and the wife comes to know more of what is involved in womanhood.[37]

But oneness is more than sexual. It denotes a blending of every aspect of a couple's lives. What Paul says in Ephesians 4:16 of the church is also true of the male and female together in marriage: "The whole body, joined and fitted together by every assisting joint, grows and builds itself up in love, when every part is working properly." As husband and wife grow together, sexually, emotionally, intellectually, and spiritually, they become the completion of the basic unit of God's creative endeavour.[38]

Unfortunately, sin entered into creation and disrupted the perfect unity of the first husband and wife. Since that time, all men and women have been flawed images of God. Thus, it sometimes happens that a particular man may believe that he is called by God to participate in His creation with a particular woman, when such is not the case. And so, a man and a woman are united in matrimony by a clergyperson, but it soon becomes evident that they are not united by God. Though they may physically become one flesh, they are not able to do so in other aspects of their lives. There is no mutuality of interests, only discord. God's gift has not been given to them as a unit. It is true that "what God has yoked together, man must not separate," but if it is only man who has done the yoking, may man not sunder it as well?[39]

Marriage as covenant. The Old Testament clearly regards marriage as a covenant, instituted and witnessed by God.[40] In fact,

---

36 Jay E. Adams, *Marriage, Divorce, and Remarriage in the Bible* (Philipsburg, NJ: Presbyterians and Reformed Publishing, 1980), 18.
37 Thomas A. Bland, "Towards a Theology of Marriage," *The Review and Expositor*, 61(1964): 10.
38 Ehrlich, 297. There is no question that, from a theological viewpoint, monogamous marriage is always God's will.
39 *Ibid.*, 308.
40 *Berith*, "covenant," is the common OT word for a variety of agreements which may include: (a) an agreement between two friends (I Sam. 18:3); (b) an agreement between two sovereigns (Gen. 21:22ff.; I Kings 5:12); (c) an agreement between a king and his subjects (II Kings 11:4); and (d) an agreement between the Lord and his people (Jer. 33:21). Recent textual finds suggest that a covenant was

the most important aspect of the wedding preliminaries was the contractual arrangement concluded by their families on behalf of the bride and groom. Provision was generally made for companionship, sustenance, and the bearing and raising of children.[41]

Marriage, moreover, was representative of the covenant — the oneness — between God and Israel. For his part, God would bless Israel and make of her a mighty nation if she, in turn, would be obedient to him. Edward Schillibeeckx writes:

> The married life of human beings, with all its ups and downs, its certainties about the past and its uncertainties about the future... all this formed the prism through which the prophets saw the saving covenant of God with his people and enabled the people to comprehend the covenant.[42]

Nor was such a covenant limited to the Old Testament. Marriage was symbolic as well of the covenant of grace between Christ and his church. Paul brings out this analogy in Ephesians 5:21–33.

Biblically, covenant carries with it a sense of permanence. It is intended as a lifelong contract. At the same time, that is not to say that a covenant can never be dissolved. In God's dealings with Israel, serious and continued violations of the covenant led to a point where he repudiated her.[43]

Covenant violation was extremely serious. It was generally a source of turmoil and suffering. It is vital, however, to realize that it could be dissolved. Moreover, once a covenant was terminated, the way was open to a new covenant. So it was in God's relationship with Judah (Jer. 31:31–34).[44]

To carry this analogy back into marriage, one may say that God

---

mediated by a third party. There were generally six elements in a covenant ceremony: (1) the preamble, giving the names of the parties; (2) a history of their relationship; (3) a basic declaration about their future relationship; (4) details of the new relationship; (5) invocation of God's witness; (6) a blessing and curse pronouncement. [J. Guhrt, "Covenant," *New International Dictionary of New Testament Theology*, 1.365–67.]

41 While there is no reference in the OT to a marriage contract *per se*, Edwin M. Yamauchi, "Cultural Aspects of Marriage in the Ancient World," *Bibliotheca Sacra*, 135 (1978): 246–47 points out that Exod. 2:10 notes a husband's obligation to his wife, while the apocryphal book, Tobit 7:14, refers to such a contract. Furthermore, several marriage contracts dating from the fifth century B.C. have been found at the Jewish garrison of Elephantine. Cf. Paul F. Palmer, "Christian Marriage: Contract or Covenant?" *Theological Studies*, 33 (1972): 617–65 who argues that marriage as a contract differs from marriage as a covenant. If so, there is a very fine line, for one cannot evade the sense of legality (or, contractuality) inherent in a covenant.

42 Eduard Schillibeeckx, *Marriage: Secular Reality and Saving Mystery*, trans. N.D. Snaith (London: Sheed and Ward, 1965), 1.61–62.

43 An exegesis of Jeremiah 3:8 will be found in the following chapter.

44 Eugene F. Roop, "Two Become One Become Two," *Brethren Life and Thought*,

has intended the marriage covenant to be permanent. Nevertheless, since the fracturing of the covenant terms by one party makes that person subject to divine judgment and frees the other party of his obligations, cannot the same thing be true of marriage?[45] The answer is that God can cause a dissolution for those who are suffering through the trauma of a marriage covenant which has been abrogated and ignored. A couple may part and go their separate ways and, in the creation of a new covenant with another, may find a new and happy life.[46]

Marriage as mutual fidelity. Marriage may be seen, above all, as "an exclusive lifelong bi-unitary community of fidelity or troth between husband and wife..."[47] A commitment to faithfulness by each partner is essential to the on-going of their married life. Such a commitment to fidelity must not be seen as the simple result of a covenantal agreement. It is unfortunate that such has been the traditional view: troth was made subservient to the marriage contract instead of being seen as a direct expression of the unique relationship between a couple which is signified in marriage.[48]

Mutual fidelity is in the truest sense rooted in Christian love. Love is a manifestation of the love of God as revealed in Christ Jesus. It is a "preferential love which includes separation and special calling."[49] In other words, one senses God's call to be joined to a certain partner and, as a consequence, unequivocally affirms, "This woman for me and no other! This man for me and no other!"[50] It is a self-sacrificing love which seeks to exist for and through one's spouse.

It is impossible for marriage partners continuously to maintain Christian love in the New testament ideal, but it is fidelity (which, as noted above, springs from that love) which brings stability and

---

(Summer 1976): 136.
45 Stott, 9.
46 Roop, 136.
47 James H. Olthuis, "Marriage," *Baker's Dictionary of Christian Ethics*, ed. Carl F.H. Henry (n.p.: Canon Press, 1973), 407 who, after such profound insight, ruins it by adding, "sealed in physical intercourse." The idea of this section, to the contrary, is to demonstrate that fidelity is the key, with or without intercourse. It is troth, not consummation, which makes a marriage. For example, if a quadriplegic man marries a physically whole woman, would his inability to consummate the marriage negate it? My contention is that it would not; their faithful exclusivity in love would make their marriage.
48 Richard Bondi, "Notes on the Theology of Marriage," *Pastoral Psychology*, 25 (Summer 1977), 302.
49 Ethelbert Stauffer, "*Agape*," *Theological Dictionary of the New Testament*, 1.48.
50 Karl Barth, *The Doctrine of Creation*, Vol. 3 of *Church Dogmatics*, trans. A.T. Mackay et al., ed. G.W. Bromiley and T.F. Torrance (Edinburgh: T. and T. Clark, 1961), 199.

permanence to their union during lapses.⁵¹ Even during those brief occasions when pride or disputes produce a loss of selfless love, the realization of loyalty and trust between partners will carry the marriage through.

It becomes evident, then, that marriage is more than a contractual arrangement. It is a matter of selfless commitment activated by a prior commitment to God in Christ. Thus, it also becomes obvious that infidelity, that which will destroy marriage, is much more than sexual. Living for oneself instead of for one's spouse is a breach of troth.⁵² One may even go so far as to say that, when the community of faithfulness dies, so does the marriage itself. And one may question whether, in God's sight, a marriage has legitimately existed, in spite of its physical consummation, if love-rooted fidelity was never there.

---

51 Ernest O. White, "The New Testament Teaching on Husband-Wife Relationships," Diss. Southern Baptist Theological Seminary, 1959, 7–71.
52 Bondi, 303 goes so far as to point to a case where the spouse gives all of his/her time to concerns outside the marriage. Cf. Patricia Beattie Jung, "A Case for Sexual Fidelity," *Word & World*, 14 (1994), 115–24.

Chapter 4

Divorce and Remarriage in the Biblical Teaching

Because Christians accept the Bible as their guide in matters of faith and practice, it is only natural to look to it for light on a matter as important as marriage or its termination. And the Bible does speak on the issues of divorce and remarriage. Contrary to what some might hold, it neither always condemns nor forbids divorce or subsequent remarriage.

The Old Testament Teaching

If one looks to the Old Testament for clear direction in regard to divorce, the result will probably be disappointment. That divorce was a common practice in ancient Hebrew society is obvious from the number of passages alluding to it (e.g. Lev. 7:7–14; Num. 30:9; Dt. 24:1–4; Hos. 2; Jer. 3:1–8). At the same time, while divorce was a custom accepted as a correct legal procedure, it was neither commended nor condemned.

In the Old Testament, divorce seems to have been the sole prerogative of the husband. Indeed, a wife might be divorced for almost any reason. Only two exceptions are to be noted. The first is in the event of a husband's falsely accusing his wife of not having been a virgin at the time of their marriage (Dt. 22:12–21). In such a case, not only was the husband forbidden ever to divorce his wife, but he was publicly chastised and forced to pay his father-in-law an indemnity of one hundred shekels of silver. The other instance resulted from a man's seduction or rape of an unattached girl (Dt. 22:28–29). Again, in addition to being never able to divorce her, he had to pay her father fifty shekels of silver.

The Mosaic Teachings

The basis of Hebrew divorce teaching is found in the Mosaic Law. Israel, like those nations around her, did not seem to have a written divorce code, but did state some of the more important provisions very briefly in writing.[1]

Deuteronomy 24:1–4. This passage seems to be based on an

---
1 David L. Lieber, "Marriage, in the Bible," *Encyclopedia Judaica*, 1971 ed.

ancient divorce law.² In its present form, it does not concern divorce in general, but prevents the remarriage of a woman to her first husband if she has, in the meantime, been the wife of another. Structurally, it is a casuistic law. The first three verses are clauses of a protasis which describes the matter under concern. Verse 4 is the apodasis, containing the resultant law. The passage reads:

> 1. If a man marries a woman and she does not find favour in his eyes because he has found some indecency in her, and he writes her out a certificate of divorce and, putting it in her hand, he sends her out from his house, 2. and if she leaves his house and becomes the wife of another man, 3. and if the second husband also turns against her and issues her a certificate of divorce, gives it to her and sends her from his house, or if he dies, 4. in such an event, the first husband who divorced her is not allowed to take her again as his wife, for she has been defiled. That would be abhorrent to the Lord. You must not bring sin on the land which the Lord your God has given you for an inheritance.

Although the passage does not deal with divorce in general, both verses 1 and 3 record a three-step procedure followed when a man divorces his wife. First, he issues her a legal certificate dissolving the marriage (*sepher keritut*, literally, "a writ of cutting off").³ Secondly, he must serve it on her ("putting it in her hand"), and thirdly, she is expelled from her husband's house. The proper steps having been taken, the promises of the marriage contract are terminated. Marriage began contractually; divorce ends it contractually.⁴

The reason given in verse 1 for the divorce is "some indecency" (*erwath dabar*) in the wife. Literally, it means "the nakedness of a thing." Perhaps it was at one time a technical legal term, but the exact meaning is no longer known.⁵ Most interpreters believe that no evidence exists to demonstrate that the term signifies adultery or some act of sexual perversity, but instead probably refers to some improper behaviour.⁶ Some further hint into its significance may also be gleaned from its use in Deuteronomy 23:12–14, where instructions

---

2 A.D.H. Mayes, *Deuteronomy, New Century Bible Commentary* (London: Oliphants, 1979), 305. For a fuller discussion of the basing of this passage on a more ancient law, see T.R. Hobbs, "Jeremiah 3:1–5 and Deuteronomy 24:1–4," *Zeitschrift fur die altetestamentliche Wissenschaft*, 86 (1974), 23–29.

3 S.R. Driver, *Deuteronomy, International Critical Commentary* (Edinburgh: T. and T. Clarke, 1895), 271. For a sample divorce bill used in later OT Judaism, see *Encyclopedia Judaica*, 6.123.

4 Jay E. Adams, *Marriage, Divorce, and Remarriage in the Bible* (Phillipsburg, NJ: Presbyterian and Reformed Publishing, 1980), 32–33.

5 Peter C. Craigie, *The Book of Deuteronomy, New International Commentary on the Old Testament* (Grand Rapids: Eerdmans, 1976), 305.

6 John Murray, *Divorce* (Philadelphia: Presbyterian and Reformed Publishing, 1961), 12 is representative. That *erwath dabar* is to be distinguished from adultery

are given for the proper disposal of bodily excrement away from the camp so that, as the Lord comes through, "he will not see among you something indecent (*erwath dabar*) and turn away from you" (23:14). The phrase would seem, therefore, to include those actions (and, perhaps, attitudes as well) by the wife which her husband found disgusting and objectionable.[7]

If, after having married another, the woman became free, either by being widowed or again divorced, her former husband was forbidden to remarry her. It has been suggested that this legislation was provided as a deterrent against a husband's hastily divorcing his wife or, if the divorce had actually occurred, he might be motivated to remarry her before it was too late.[8] There may have been, however, a stronger safeguard against a hasty divorce, a financial one. Although the Old Testament makes no explicit mention of it, evidence suggests that, in the event that a husband divorced his wife, he was obliged to return the *mohar*, or "brideprice."[9]

The deuteronomic account gives as the reason for the prohibition against marrying the same husband that, by her second marriage, the woman has been defiled; a marriage again to her former husband would be "abhorrent to the Lord" (v. 4).

One may well ask in what sense such a defilement has occurred. There are many suggestions. One interpreter intimates that the second marriage is a defilement of the woman tantamount to adultery in that she has been polluted by the *emissio semenis* of sexual intercourse with the new husband.[10] Another holds a similar view

---

or fornication is evidenced by the fact that the extreme penalty was executed for those sins, namely, stoning to death (Dt. 22:20–24). Thus, a wife guilty of sexual infidelity would not be divorced, but executed. As to how long the capital penalty was carried out is a question, for nowhere in the OT does one find it enacted, although numerous cases of adultery are cited (e.g. Gen. 38:26; Jud. 19:2–3; II Sam. 12:13–14; Hos. 3:1). Indeed, by the time of the writing of Prov. 6:24–35, an affair with an adulterous woman was regarded as similar to an affair with a prostitute.

7 The rabbinic interpretations of *erwath dabar* will be examined in the section on NT teachings.
8 Driver, 272.
9 Such a convention (and frequently the money itself) was known as *ketubbah*. David R. Mace, *Hebrew Marriage, A Sociological Study* (New York: Philosophical Library, 1953), 253 notes that it is mentioned both by the Code of Hammurabi and in the Mishnah, and that it may have escaped mention by the OT writers "because, as in the Babylonian Code, it was stated as an amount equivalent to the mohar." Cf. Millard Burrows, *The Basis of Israelite Marriage* (New Haven, CT: American Oriental Society, 1938), 63–65 and Leonard Swidler, *Women in Judaism* (Metuchen, NJ: Scarecrow Press, 1976), 157–59.
10 C.F. Keil and Franz Delitzsch, *Biblical Commentary on the Old Testament*, trans. James R. Martin (Grand Rapids: Eerdmans, 1950), 3.418.

that, by divorcing his wife and then remarrying her, the first husband has prostituted her and then acted as her procurer, thus contaminating her body.[11] The adultery concept is also put forth, namely, that the divorce did not really annul the former marriage and so, by going to another man, the wife is fracturing her vows to her first husband.[12] Still another declares that the idea here is a desire to prevent serial divorce and remarriage, a legalized form of adultery.[13]

The major problem with trying to explain defilement as tantamount to adultery is that the text itself militates against it. The defilement has nothing to do with the second marriage itself, but pertains solely to the former husband's potential relationship with the woman. The idea is perhaps best expressed by the *New English Bible*, which renders the passage, "She has become for him unclean." It appears likely that the above commentators are interpreting the text with Jesus' statements on divorce and remarriage in mind.

It has been suggested that the reason for the prohibition is to protect a second marriage from a jealous first husband who has decided that he wants his wife back and is willing to disrupt her new marriage in order to get her.[14] Thus, contrary to condemning the second marriage, the legislation goes to great lengths to protect it by declaring the woman unclean from her former husband, and such a possibility as remarriage to him to be "an abomination" or "abhorrent". Theologian Gordon Wenham enlarges upon this idea by explaining that, according to the levitical incest laws, marriage creates a familial relationship; through wedlock, a woman joins her husband's family and so becomes a sister to him and his brothers. Consequently, if the marriage is terminated for any reason, neither the husband nor his brothers can remarry her.[15]

The incest explanation, however, fails to take into account the significance of the second marriage, which is what lies behind the prohibition of the first husband's remarrying his former wife. Following the reasoning for the incest theory, there would not really

---

11 John Calvin, *Commentaries on the Last Four Books of Moses*, trans. Chas. W. Bingham (Grand Rapids:Eerdmans, 1950), 3.94.
12 Clyde T. Francisco, *The Book of Deuternomy* (Grand Rapids: Baker Books, 1964), 89. He does not explain how she could default when the divorce was her husband's initiative and she had no control over it.
13 Craigie, 305 although why such a practice should be necessary, given polygamy, is questionable.
14 R. Yaron, "The Restoration of Marriage," *Journal of Jewish Studies*, 30 (1966), 8.
15 Gordon W. Wenham, "The Restoration of Marriage Reconsidered," *Journal of Jewish Studies*, 30 (1979), 40. Cf. Gordon Wenham, "Marriage and Divorce in the Old Testament," *Didaskalia*, 1 (November 1989), 11.

be any significance to future marriages, but instead to the divorce itself. Once being divorced from his wife, for the man to marry her again (according to this line of thinking) would be incestuous, regardless of any intervening marriages.[16]

In the final analysis, one must confess ignorance as to the meaning of "defilement" and how it is "abhorrent to the Lord." The legalities here rest on ancient cultic foundations which were clear in the time of the writer, but which since have become obscure.[17]

The concluding phrase of the law (v. 4) declares that such a prohibited remarriage would bring sin on the land. Some scholars declare that this reference is a later, postexilic, addition based on Jeremiah 3:1, where the land is considered polluted as a result of the breaking of this law.[18] Such an assumption is unfounded, for the concept of the land and its relationship to God was always an important one to Israel. The land is seen as the heritage of the Lord. The Israelites are only sojourners (Lev. 25:23), stewards of his possessions. The land is holy because God is holy. Disobedience is a violation of his land.[19] Sexual sins are especially linked to its defilement (e.g. Lev. 18:25; Num. 5:3; Hos. 4:3; Jer. 16:18). It is highly probable that, as with the earlier section of this law, the warning against polluting the land goes back well beyond the time of writing, and rests on an ancient cultic saga.[20]

Deuteronomy 24:1–4, then, does not deal with divorce as such. It neither commends nor condemns the action. Its intention is an ordered society and the protection of women. Far from condemning remarriage, it regulates it, and seeks to ensure its stability and wellbeing.

Other pertinent passages. One case of divorce mentioned in Genesis 21:9–14 is that of Abraham and Hagar. Because Sarah had no son, she gave her slave, Hagar, to Abraham as a second wife. Following the birth of Isaac, however, Sarah wished to minimize any possible threat to his inheritance rights and so she urged Abraham to repudiate Hagar and her son (by Abraham), Ishmael. Abraham, to his credit, hesitated to do so until God intervened with assurances that he should (21:11–13). It was then that Hagar and Ishmael were

---

16 Harold Ray England, "Divorce and Remarriage in I Corinthians 7:10–16," Diss. Southern Baptist Theological Seminary, 1982, 35–36.
17 Gerhard von Rad, *Deuteronomy, Old Testament Library* (Philadelphia: Westminster Press, 1966), 150.
18 Mayes, 323.
19 M. Ottosson, "*eretz*," *Theological Dictionary of the Old Testament*, 1.401–02.
20 von Rad, 150.

expelled from Abraham's camp (a *de facto* divorce).[21]

The book of Leviticus 22:7, 14 cites two cases where a particular group of people may not marry a divorced woman. The first is the priests: "They must not marry a prostitute or a woman who has lost her virginity, nor shall they marry a woman divorced from her husband; for the priest is holy to his God" (v. 7).[22] Purity was paramount for a priest because of his special service to the Lord. Therefore, women who had had previous sexual experience were excluded as objects of matrimony. Only those who had preserved their virginity were permitted to be the wife of a priest.[23] The high priest was even more restricted: not only did he have to marry a virgin, but a virgin "of his own people" (v. 14). Because he was the chosen one of all his brothers, it was even more important that his holiness be assured along with the purity of his children. Should he fail to marry a virgin, there would be a possibility that their first child might not be of the priestly line (that is, the woman might already be pregnant with someone else's child).[24] A prospective wife would, in addition, have to be from the high priest's own tribe to assure purity of race.

Some have taken these passages as evidence that women who were divorced were being compared unfavourably with their peers,

---

21 Johannes Pedersen, *Israel* (London: Oxford Univ. Press, 1926), 2.70.
22 There have been differences of opinion on the proper rendering of this verse. The NIV reads, "They must not marry women defiled by prostitution or divorced from their husbands,..." The NASB reads in a similar vein. The RSV makes a slight, but significant, shift: "They shall not marry a harlot or a woman who has been defiled, neither shall they marry a woman who has been divorced from her husband,..." The NEB makes a substantial change from the above: "A priest shall not marry a prostitute or a girl who has lost her virginity, nor shall he marry a woman divorced from her husband,..." The crux of the problem lies in *wihalalah* (from the root *halal*, which has been rendered variously as "defiled" or "deflowered"). The NIV and NASB have omitted the conjunction. Furthermore, the only meaning given by Gerhard Lisowsky, ed., *Konkordanz zum Hebraischen Alten Testament*, 2nd ed. (Stuttgart: Deutsche Bibelgesellschaft, 1981), 499 for this word (which appears in this form in v. 7 alone) is "pierced", which would best suit the NEB rendition.
23 A. Noordtzij, *Leviticus, Bible Student's Commentary*, trans. Raymond Togtman (Grand Rapids: Zondervan, 1982), 217. Cf. Martin Noth, *Leviticus, Old Testament Library* (London: SCM Press, 1965), 156 who says, "...only a woman widowed by the death of her husband is, by wording of v. 7a, excepted from this rule...." But Noth argues from silence and is contradicted by Ezek. 44:22, which denies widows (excepting the widow of a priest) and stresses that a priest may marry only a virgin.
24 Gordon J. Wenham, *The Book of Leviticus, New International Commentary on the Old Testament* (Grand Rapids: Eerdmans, 1979), 292.

that divorce carried with it a stigma.[25] If so, then the argument would have to be extended, logically, to include widows. But it is highly dubious that the writer's intention is to impugn either. It is more likely that he is simply emphasizing the necessity for sexual purity; that is, the bride must be virginal. Such a requirement was fully in line with the fact that the holiness code was much more demanding of the priests and the high priest than of ordinary Israelites.

Prophetic Teachings

Prophetic teaching on divorce is no more revealing than that of Moses. Most of what the prophets have to say is bound up in the symbolism of marriage as representative of God's dealings with his people.

Jeremiah 3:1-8. In this passage, Judah is depicted as a faithless wife who, even though she has forfeited all legal claim on her husband, still expects him to overlook her peccadilloes.[26] The first verse is reminiscent of Deuteronomy 24:1-4. It may be that the prophet was familiar with that passage and was using it as a foundation for his invective,[27] or it may be that both he and the deuteronomic writer were drawing on an older version of the legislation no longer available:[28]

> Suppose that a man should divorce his wife, and she should leave him and become the wife of another, can he go back to her again?[29] Would not the land be completely polluted? But you have played the harlot with many lovers. And would you now return to me?[30] says the Lord.

If the Law forbade a woman's return to her former husband, how could the Lord be expected to receive back one whose brazen harlotry had been manifested in every conceivable place?[31] Judah's desire for perversion was insatiable: "Where have you not been

---

25 So Abel Isaksson, *Marriage and Ministry in the New Temple* (Copenhagen: Lund, 1965), 37.
26 John Bright, *Jeremiah, The Anchor Bible* (Garden City, NY: Doubleday, 1965), 25.
27 J.A. Thompson, *The Book of Jeremiah, New International Commentary on the Old Testament* (Grand Rapids: Eerdmans, 1980), 190.
28 Hobbs, 24.
29 The Masoretic text and LXX do not agree on this clause. The LXX reads, "Can she go back to him again?" The MT is more likely correct, for that is the sense of Dt. 24:4. The initiative of both marriage and divorce was the man's.
30 There is some question as to whether this clause is to be translated as a question ("Would you now return...?") or as a jussive ("Let her return...."). Considering the use of divorce imagery, the former seems more appropriate. But, cf. Charles L. Feinberg, *Jeremiah, A Commentary* (Grand Rapids: Zondervan, 1982), 14.
31 Roy L. Honeycutt, Jr., *Jeremiah, Witness Under Pressure* (Nashville: Convention Press, 1981), 14.

debauched?" (v. 2).

Because of her depravity, God caused a drought. Neither the showers nor the spring rains fell (v. 3). But these efforts to bring the nation to repentance were unsuccessful. Judah remained totally without shame. In verses 4 and 5, Jeremiah draws a dichotomy between Judah's profession and her actions: "My father,[32] you are the dear bridegroom of my youth... This is how you talk, but you have done all the evil you were able." The Hebrew word for "bridegroom" has a number of meanings, such as friend, companion, husband, family head, and the term may have been deliberately chosen by Jeremiah, for it communicated the broad range of function that Yahweh had provided since Israel's youth, and which she refused to recognize.[33]

The prophet then turns to (the Northern Kingdom of) Israel. He refers to her as apostasy personified; the Hebrew term literally means "apostasy Israel." Israel, like Judah, has played the harlot at every turn (v. 6). Judah observed Israel's behaviour, and had seen how these actions had led to divorce.[34] God had hoped that Israel would return to him, but she did not (v.7). Therefore, he repudiated her by giving her a certificate of divorce (*sepher keritut*), and had sent her on her way (v. 8).

According to verse 6, this passage was written in the days of Josiah (*c*. 622 B.C.), about a century after the destruction of the Northern Kingdom at the hands of the Assyrians.[35] God had dissolved his covenant with her and had cast her off as a righteous man would divorce an unfaithful wife. Judah, warns the prophet, is in imminent danger of the same fate.

While Jeremiah mentions the underlying cause of adultery, his emphasis is really on the basis of commitment. Because Israel broke her commitment to the Lord, their relationship was cut apart and the marriage was terminated. No condemnation of divorce is found here. Indeed, one may say that, theologically, God is pictured as a divorced person! Jeremiah notes in verses 6–8 that He followed the legal

---

32 It was not unusual for a young bride to address her older husband in the familiar form, *'ab*.
33 Thompson, 192–93.
34 Andrew W. Blackwood, Jr., *Commentary on Jeremiah* (Waco, TX: Word Books, 1977), 57.
35 The origin of vv. 6ff. is much debated. Within a poetic section has been inserted this prose passage which changes the figure of speech: Jeremiah generally uses "Israel" to denote the whole community of faith; here, it refers to the Northern Kingdom. For varying views of the origin of the passage, see Blackwood, 57; Bright, 26–27; James P. Hyatt, "The Book of Jeremiah," *The Interpreter's Bible*, 5.825–26.

procedure described in Deuteronomy 24:1–4.

Hosea 2:2–3. The purpose of the book of Hosea is to show God's love for Israel as analogous to Hosea's love for Gomer. Just as Gomer played the harlot, so did Israel. Just as Gomer broke her marriage contract with Hosea by her sexual infidelity, so Israel violated the covenant with God through her spiritual infidelities. At the same time, through Hosea's continuing love for Gomer, God's redeeming love for Israel shines forth.[36]

Because of the marriage analogy, one finds many allusions to divorce in this book. It has been suggested that verse 2 contains an ancient divorce formula: "She is not my wife and I am not her husband."[37] In this instance, it is used as the writer's declaration to repudiate his wife, an action witnessed by her children and open to public scrutiny.[38] The scene is allegorical and refers to God's intention to repudiate Israel.[39]

In verse 3, Hosea threatens to strip his wife naked, a reference to the custom of ancient times where a husband publicly stripped his wife as a sign of her adultery.[40]

There is considerable question as to whether an actual divorce took place between Hosea and Gomer,[41] but there are numerous references to the practice and it is certainly threatened. Nor can anyone find any condemnation of divorce here. Indeed, once again it is the Lord threatening to dissolve his marriage with Israel. One cannot, however, fail to note the heartbreak and pathos of the broken relationship. Furthermore, one finds here a consideration of how far love is willing to go in order to preserve marriage.[42]

Malachi 2:10–16. The book of Malachi initially is concerned with the sins of the priests. The prophet accuses them of profaning the Temple, abusing the covenant with Levi, and, by turning away from the Lord, causing many to stumble. Then, beginning with verse 10,

---

36 Dwight Hervey Small, "The Prophet Hosea: God's Alternative to Divorce for the Reason of Infidelity," *Journal of Psychology and Theology*, 7 (Summer 1979), 134.
37 John Paterson, "Divorce and Desertion in the Old Testament," *Journal of Biblical Literature*, 51 (1932), 166. But, cf. James A. Ward, *Hosea: A Theological Commentary* (New York: Harper and Row, 1966), 25.
38 Ward, *Hosea*, 29.
39 Ward, *Hosea*, 29. Francis I. Anderson and Donald Noel Freedman, *Hosea, Anchor Bible* (Garden City, NY: Doubleday, 1980), 222 stress that "it is not possible to fit the clean break of a divorce in with the other things that are happening in this discourse." Hosea here uses the language of reconciliation, not repudiation.
40 Robert Gordis, *Poets, Prophets, and Sages* (Bloomington, IN: Indiana Univ. Press, 1971), 249–50, n. 30a. Some ancient cultures used this practice as a public divorce ceremony, although Israel did not.
41 See n. 40, above.
42 England, 49.

he turns his attention to all the people. They, too, are guilty of treachery against the Lord. The most obvious sin, he declares, is their repudiation of the Hebrew wife of their youth in favour of a heathen woman.[43]

The pericope is not an easy one to examine, for it is filled with fractured phraseology and obscure references. Scholars have attempted to deal with the problem by emending the text or deleting portions of it but, as one scholar has noted, "It is always perilous to presume what a prophet would or would not have written."[44]

The passage may be broken down into three subsections, all of which have the underlying theme of treachery in relationships. Verse 10 concerns treachery towards each other; verses 11–13 deal with treachery towards God; and verses 14–16 are involved with treachery towards one's spouse.[45]

The prophet begins with basic principles. Israel is a people chosen, guided, and ruled by God. He is both their Creator and Father.[46] Since all Jews are children of God, then every violation against one's fellow, such as that of a Jew repudiating his Hebrew wife for a foreign woman, is an offence against God and a desecration of his covenant (v. 10).[47]

The following verses clearly define the ways in which the Jews have violated God's covenant: "Judah has dealt treacherously and an abomination has been committed in Israel; for Judah has profaned the holiness of Yahweh, because he has loved and married the daughter of a foreign god" (v. 11).[48] The marriage of Jews to pagan

---

43 There were numerous problems with pagan intermarriage during and after the Exile. Both Nehemiah (13:3ff.) and Ezra (10:2ff.) condemned the Jews for marrying foreigners and for giving their children to them in marriage. Ezra went so far as to command that all Jews who were married to pagan women divorce and send them away.

44 Page H. Kelley, "A Commentary on the Prophecy of Malachi," Diss. Southern Baptist Theological Seminary, 1952, 111.

45 Théophane Chary, *AggéeZecharieMalachi* (Paris: Librairie Lecoffre, 1969), 255.

46 Chary, 256. Douglas R. Jones, *Haggai, Zechariah, and Malachi, Torch Bible Commentary* (London: SCM Press, 1962), 194 states that "the sense of the whole passage requires that the ONE FATHER is Abraham." In so saying, he follows a number of commentators (e.g. Jerome, Sanctius, Calvin). But Abraham is precluded by virtue of having fathered other nations beside Israel. And God, furthermore, refers to himself as "father" in 1:6.

47 C. F. Keil and Franz Delitzsch, *The Twelve Minor Prophets, Biblical Commentary on the Old Testament* (Grand Rapids: Eerdmans, 1949), 448. Cf. Beth Glazier McDonald, "Intermarriage, Divorce and the *bat'el nekar*," *Journal of Biblical Literature*, 106 (December 1987), 610.

48 Most versions render "holiness" as "sanctuary". For discussions on both, see Jones, 195, and John M.P. Smith, *Malachi, International Critical Commentary* (New York: Chas. Scribner's Sons, 1912), 49.

women is an abomination, a grave attack both on the holiness of all the people and on that cultus itself. The purity of Israel's faith, already corrupted by the vile practices of the priests, is being further compromised by introducing into Jewish society wives and mothers who are ignorant of the Lord and who do not follow him.[49] Malachi's reference to "the daughter of a foreign god" emphasizes that these women were actually idolatresses;[50] they were active in the pursuit of false gods. In verse 12, he warns that God will destroy the offspring of the one who desecrates the holiness of the Lord by union with a foreign woman. Furthermore, such a man will find no one in Israel to represent him or help him.[51] Because of their great wickedness, when these disobedient Jews flock to the altar to seek the Lord's favour, albeit with weeping, he will reject their worship.[52]

In verse 14, the prophet tells the Jews why the Lord does not accept their offering: he has witnessed their treachery against their wife of the covenant, against the wife of their youth. Double treachery is obvious in the breaking of both the marriage contract and the covenant of God.[53] The allusion to "the wife of your youth" suggests that the older Hebrew wives who had shared the hard times of exile with their husbands were now being divorced for younger heathen women. While polygamy was acceptable, and there was, ostensibly, no good reason why the first wife could not have been retained along with a second, monogamy was the prevailing condition in most Jewish families after the Exile. It may very well have been that the divorce of the first wife was a prerequisite to the second marriage required by the family of the prospective new bride, for the first wife always held the place of power.[54]

Verse 15 has been called "the most obscure verse in the book of Malachi."[55] There is little scholarly agreement as to its meaning. Most translations have been based on emendations of the text, but few of the emenders agree.[56] The aim of the verse may, however, be seen in the last part: "... let no one deal treacherously with the wife of his

---

49 Robert C. Dentan, "The Book of Malachi," *The Interpreter's Bible* (Nashville: Abingdon Press, 1956), 6.1134.
50 Kelley, 115.
51 T. Miles Bennett, "Malachi," *The Broadman Commentary* (Nashville, TN: Broadman Press, 1972), 7.385.
52 Kelley, 120 notes that Jewish commentators regard the tears of v. 13 to be those of the rejected Jewish wives who came to the altar to pour out their grief, but such a view does not fit the context (especially of the following verse).
53 Jones, 196.
54 Smith, 52.
55 John M.P. Smith, "A Note on Malachi 2:15a," *American Journal of Semitic Languages and Literature*, 28 (1911–12), 204.
56 Kelley, 124. See 124–28 for a selection of scholarly renditions.

youth."

The sixteenth verse is cited by many as a prooftext of "a general truth which is found nowhere else in the O.T., that God is opposed to divorce."[57] God says, "I hate divorce,[58] and him who covers his garment with violence." One must ask, though, whether the Lord is making a universal declaration on divorce or if he is making a specific statement on divorce in the context of those who dismiss their wives for younger women or more advantageous alliances. The latter seems more probable.

The expression, "him who covers his garment with violence," is unique to this passage. It seems to refer to violent and unjust actions against the marriage relationship.[59]

The divorce passage is concluded with the warning: "So take heed to yourselves that you are not faithless." The Lord will not countenance this multifaceted treachery.

Conclusions

When one looks to the Old Testament for an insight into divorce, it becomes evident that very little help will be forthcoming. None of the passages examined either advocate or forbid divorce. Nonetheless, divorce is a live option. Jeremiah reveals that God had divorced Israel and reserved the prerogative to divorce Judah as well. The same possibility is revealed by Hosea. At the same time, divorce is not an obligation. The book of Hosea contains God's offer of love and forgiveness. Reconciliation is held out, conditional upon repentance. Hosea is indicative that, while divorce may be possible, love is a better way.

The New Testament Teaching

There are four New Testament books that contain teachings on divorce and remarriage. The earliest seems to be Paul, in 1 Corinthians 7.[60] The remaining three are the Synoptic Gospels: Matthew has two accounts (5:31,32, and 19:3–12); Mark and Luke, one each (Mk. 10:1–12 and Lk. 16:18)[61] Although all five passages are

---

57 Dentan, 1136. So also Jones, Chary, and Dods.
58 The text actually reads, "He ...," but it has been changed by most translators to harmonize with the context of a direct quotation.
59 David C. Jones, "Malachi on Divorce," *Prebyterion*, 15 (Spring 1989), 22.
60 Leon Morris,*The First Epistle of Paul to the Corinthians, Tyndale NT Commentaries* (Grand Rapids: Eerdmans, 1958), 29 places the letter in the midfifties A.D., as do the majority of translators.
61 Jack Dean Kingsbury, *Jesus Christ in Matthew, Mark, and Luke, Proclamation Commentaries* (Philadelphia: Fortress Press, 1981) represents the bulk of scholarly

based on the teachings of Jesus, there are striking differences among them. The task here will be to examine each one in an effort to determine what it says, why the accounts differ, and then to apply them to our own situation.

The Synoptic Teachings

While there are four Synoptic accounts, they appear to be derived from only two sources. The first is the basis for what one finds in Matthew 5:31-32 and Luke 16:18.[62] The other is the basis for Mark 10:1-12 and Matthew 19:3-12, and is placed in the context of a controversy between Jesus and the Pharisees.[63]

Matthew 5:31-32. Matthew has made this saying one of six antitheses found in the Sermon on the Mount. Among them, it stands out by way of introduction. Whereas the other five antitheses begin with, "You have heard it said...," this one is introduced, "It was said..." It is, furthermore, the only saying taken from Deuteronomy, the others coming from Exodus and Leviticus. Because of its context following the saying on adultery, it would seem that Matthew inserted it as a supplementary comment on the adultery teaching.[64] It reads:

> And it was said, Whoever divorces (*apoluse*) his wife, let him give her a certificate of divorce. But I tell you that whoever divorces his wife apart from a matter of unchastity, makes her commit adultery; and whoever shall marry a divorced woman commits adultery.

The word used here for "divorce" comes from *apoluo*. The classical use of the word denotes the releasing of prisoners or the freeing of a person from legal charges, and it is used occasionally of dismissing a wife. In the *Septuagint*, it is used of a variety of things, including divorce. In the New Testament, it refers to the release of a prisoner, to send people away, to dismiss from military service and, especially, to the divorcing of a wife.[65]

It may be well to ask what is meant in this passage by "commits adultery." The word *moicheia* ("adultery") refers essentially to a

---

opinion on the dates for the Synoptics as: about A.D.70 for Mark (p. 54), A.D.85 for Luke (p. 124), and A.D.90 for Matthew (p. 86). For a more conservative view of the Synoptic dates, see Dale Moody, "A New Chronology for the New Testament," *Review and Expositor* 78 (Spring, 1982): 211-232.

62 The majority of scholars would refer to this source as that tradition commonly called Q.
63 It is regarded by many as Marcan tradition.
64 Jacques Dupont, *Mariage et divorce dans l'Evangile: Matthieu 19:3-12 et parallèles* (Bruges: Desclée et Brouwer, 1959), 46.
65 I. Howard Marshall, "Divorce," *New International Dictionary of New Testament Theology*, 1.505-06.

violation of the marriage covenant.[66] In the Old Testament, it involves the violation of the marriage with another (cf. Gen. 39:10ff., Lev. 20:10). It is possible only if intercourse has occurred between a man and a betrothed or married Hebrew woman. Thus, while the Old Testament Hebrew male is not obliged to avoid all extramarital sex, the married woman must be totally faithful to her husband. The reasoning here is that, in marriage, the woman becomes the property of her husband.[67] In the New Testament, Jesus makes a radical shift which denies the husband sexual licence and brings a measure of equality to the wife. Both are obligated to marital fidelity.[68] One may go even farther to say that the prohibition of adultery is not restricted only to the negative avoidance of a wrong sexual act. It is fulfilled only in the total and loving commitment of each spouse to the other.[69]

Matthew, in this passage, considers the matter of adultery from the male point of view. The husband is responsible above all, for it is he who initiates the divorce.[70] By divorcing his wife, except on the ground of unfaithfulness on her part,[71] he forces her to remarry[72] (she must, simply in order to survive economically!), and the unity of flesh with him (that is, the first husband) will be violated (a fracturing of God's lifelong intent as described by Gen. 2:24). In the same way, the man who marries her will be committing adultery against her first husband.[73]

Luke 16:18. Luke has inserted this saying between the parable of

---

66 Adams, 54.
67 Friedrich Hauck, "*moicheuô, ktl.,*" *Theological Dictionary of the New Testament*, 4.730.
68 Hauck, 733.
69 Hauck, 734. Jesus makes this clear when he warns in Mt. 5:28 that the lustful look is as adulterous as the act itself.
70 B.N. Wambacq, "Matthieu 5, 31–32," *Nouvelle Revue Théologique*, 104 (Jan.-Feb. 1982), 42.
71 The "exception clause" will be discussed in detail, below, in the section on Mt. 19:9.
72 Frank Stagg, "Matthew," *The Broadman Commentary* (Nashville, TN: Broadman Press, 1969), 8.110 believes that the Greek does not justify the translation "causes her to commit adultery," because the of passive infinitive, *moicheusthenai*, which he says is untranslatable in English, although something like "made adulterous" or "victimized with respect to adultery" would be close. He declares that one cannot understand Jesus to suggest "that an innocent wife" is an adulteress because her husband divorces her. Exegetes usually assume that she remarries, but this is only a deduction from the next clause." In fact, George R. Ewald, *Jesus and Divorce* (Waterloo, ON: Herald Press, 1991), 33–34 stipulates that a divorced woman became her own mistress, subject neither to her (former) husband nor her father, and might give herself in marriage to whomever she chose.
73 It is interesting that Matthew here relates divorce *per se*, rather than marriage, to the commission of adultery.

the shrewd manager and the parable of Lazarus and the rich man. It follows the account of the Pharisees' derisive reaction to Jesus' teaching, probably to serve as an illustration of the difference between their teaching and his own. Luke's version reads: "Everyone who divorces his wife and marries another commits adultery, and he who marries her who has been divorced from a husband, commits adultery."

Jesus declares that the man who remarries following divorce is entering an adulterous relationship, as is the man who marries a divorced woman. The saying is not unlike that of Matthew 5:32, although there is one significant difference: Matthew holds that the man who divorces his wife causes her to become an adulteress, whereas Luke finds the man guilty of adultery if he remarries.[74]

The obvious difference between these two sayings, both from the same source, dictates some examination as to which may more fully represent Jesus' original saying. There are scholars who claim Luke's version as the more primitive form, using the principles of similarity and dissimilarity in their decision.[75] While some, for example, regard the phrase, "and marries another" (Lk. 16:18b), as a Lucan addition, the fact that it is present in all other forms except Matthew 5:32 would suggest that it is a part of the original saying. On the other hand, the expression, "and he who marries her who has been divorced commits adultery" (Lk. 16:18c), since it is not present in Paul or Mark, is possibly a later addition. Thus, "the chances are the most primitive form of the logion is preserved here in Lk. 16:18a–b."[76] It might also be said that Luke testifies to a more ancient tradition because he is more concerned with preserving the saying itself than with a particular context.[77]

Opinion, however, is by no means unanimous. Many scholars opt for the Matthean priority, observing that, because "Matthew looks at it entirely from a male standpoint, ...it may be assumed that Matthew is closer to what a Palestinian Jesus... may have said."[78] There is evident dissent, and conclusive proof for one position or another is impossible.

Mark 10:1–12. Both Mark 10:1–12 and Matthew 19:3–12 appear to

---

74 I. Howard Marshall, *The Gospel of Luke, A Commentary on the Greek Text* (Exeter: Paternoster Press, 1978), 631.
75 Joseph A. Fitzmyer, "The Matthean Divorce texts and Some New Palestinian Evidence," *Journal of Theological Studies*, 37 (1976), 200.
76 Fitzmyer, 201–02. Cf. B.H. Streeter, *The Four Gospels* (London: MacMillan, 1930), 287.
77 Dupont, 48.
78 Bruce Vawter, *On Genesis, A New Reading* (Garden City, NY: Doubleday, 1977), 530–31.

come from the same source, for they are parallel in much of their structural arrangement, teaching, and context. The Marcan version is composite and consists of a pronouncement story (10:2–9) and a dominical saying (10:10–12).[79] Thus, Mark is actually providing two sayings of Jesus on divorce.

The first section is set in the context of a dispute with the Pharisees. Jesus has just returned from Galilee and, as always, is teaching a large crowd of people (v. 1). The Pharisees question him:[80] "And the Pharisees, coming up, questioned him in order to test him, 'Is it lawful for a man to divorce his wife?'" (v. 2). Some have questioned the authenticity of the passage on the ground that Mark makes the Pharisees ask a question which no Pharisee would ask, namely, whether divorce is legitimate.[81] It is true that the Jews overwhelmingly accepted divorce as a right prescribed by Mosaic Law. On the other hand, if the questioning of Jesus occurred at Peraea, it may have been an effort to force him to express himself, as had John the Baptist, on the marriage of Herod Antipas to Herodias, the former wife of Philip, Antipas' halfbrother.[82] Peraea was a part of the Tetrarch's territory and they would have been able to count on his support against Jesus.

The Lord recognizes that the question is one of legal interpretation and, in proper rabbinical form,[83] counters with a question of his own: "What did Moses command you?" (v. 3). Their response? "Moses allowed the writing of a certificate of divorce and dismissal (*apolusai*)." It is clear that Moses did not *command* divorce and the Pharisees knew that well, which is the reason for their response in such a fashion: "Moses allowed...."[84] Jesus, therefore, takes their confession and turns it upon them, declaring that such

---

79 Fitzmyer, 204.
80 Many authorities omit *proselthontes hoi Pharisaioi* (e.g. D, i[a,b,d,k,r], syr, origen). Robert H. Gundry, *Matthew, A Commentary on His Literary and Theological Art* (Grand Rapids: Eerdmans, 1982), 376 alleges that, while external evidence may favour its inclusion, the strong possibility of Matthean influence on copyists of Mark would favour its omission [cf. Bruce Metzger, *A Textual Commentary on the Greek New Testament* (New York: United Bible Societies, 1971), 104]. If the omission stands, then it is the people who put the question to Jesus, and Matthew had adapted the teaching to suit his own theological ends.
81 So Charles, 29–30.
82 John Bowman, *The Gospel of Mark, Studia PostBiblica* (Leiden: E.J. Brill, 1965), 209. Cf. Donald W. Shaner, *A Christian View of Divorce According to the New Testament* (Leiden: E.J. Brill, 1969), 38. It may be that the Herodians accompanied the Pharisees. It had happened before (Mk. 8:15; 12:13).
83 David Daube, *The New Testament and Rabbinic Judaism* (London: Athlone Press, 1956), 146ff. presents a compelling argument for Jesus' use of rabbinic techniques, public retort and private reflection, precept and example, in this divorce passage.
84 Dupont, 18.

permission is only a concession to human hardheartedness: "He wrote this command out of regard to your hardheartedness (*sklerokardian*)" (v. 5). The word *skleros* means "hard" in the sense of "rough" or "coarse" rather than "unimpressionable", and *kardia* is the common New Testament word for the inner self.[85]

Jesus recognizes the legality of divorce, but he seeks to restore the divine intention for men and women as found initially. Instead of basing marriage on the creation of woman for man, he emphasizes the fuller ground of the unity of their relationship:

> 6.But from the beginning of creation God made them male and female. 7.Because of this, a man shall leave his father and mother and be joined to his wife, 8.and the two shall become one flesh; so that they are no longer two, but one.

The Pharisees had trouble with this divine concept of marriage, for they saw husband and wife as two (similar to master and servant); thus, a husband could divorce his wife on any pretext at any time.[86]

Verse 9 sums up Jesus' pronouncement on the subject of marriage and divorce in Mark: "What, therefore (*oun*), God has yoked together, man should not separate (*chorizetœ*)." *Oun* introduces the statement as an accurate deduction from the early Scriptures of what God intends for marriage.[87] The verb, *chorizœ* ("separate"), is a term used in a legal sense both in the papyri and by Paul as a synonym for divorce.[88] Marriage is not just a manmade institution. It is a holy union created by God himself and man must not tamper with it.[89]

The remainder of the Marcan teaching (vv. 10–12) is a dominical saying set in the context of Jesus' giving the disciples further revelation in light of his criticism of the Pharisees' interpretation of Moses (v. 10): "And he said to them, 'Whoever shall divorce (*apolusˆ*) his wife and marry another, commits adultery with her. And if a woman shall divorce her husband and marry another, she commits adultery'" (vv. 11–12). Like Luke 16:18, this passage attributes more guilt to subsequent remarriage than to the divorce itself. Verse 12 has been a source of controversy. Many scholars see it as an addition that Mark has put into Jesus' mouth to accord with actual conditions

---

85 Ezra P. Gould, *The Gospel According to Saint Mark*, International Critical Commentary (Edinburgh: T. and T. Clark, 1896), 184.
86 R.C.H. Lenski, *The Interpretation of St. Mark's Gospel* (Minneapolis: Augsburg, 1946), 418.
87 Lenski, 419.
88 Shaner, 40. See section on "Pauline Teachings" for a fuller explanation of *chôrizo*.
89 A.E.J. Rawlinson, *Saint Mark*, Westminster Commentaries (London: Methuen, 1925), 135 believes that while, in the Greek the word "man" in antithesis to "God" might refer generally to "any human authority," the man who is thinking about trying to separate what "God has yoked together" is undoubtedly the husband.

outside of Jewry.⁹⁰ On the other hand, there is good reason to believe that Jesus did say it, especially in view of Mark's emphasis on the Herodians working hand-in-hand with the Pharisees to discredit Him. It may well be that Jesus was alluding to Herodias who was perhaps divorced under Roman law to marry Antipas.⁹¹ Jesus, undoubtedly aware of current events, surely knew that such things were occurring in the Roman world.⁹²

Matthew 19:3–12 and the meaning of the "exception clause". The Matthean location of this passage is, unlike Mark, clearly set in Judaea. Those who dispute with Jesus are obviously Pharisees. While not questioning the legitimacy of divorce, they did debate the grounds for such an action. The rabbinic schools of Hillel and Shammai argued over the significance of *erwath dabar*, "some indecency". The Mishnah summarizes these views:

> The School of Shammai say: A man may not divorce his wife unless he has found unchastity in her, for it is written, *Because he hath found in her indecency in anything*. And the School of Hillel say: (He may divorce her) even if she spoiled a dish for him, for it is written, *Because he hath found in her indecency in anything*.⁹³

The Shammaites were rigorists. They held that *erwath dabar* signified sexual immorality and that no other cause was legitimate.⁹⁴ Hillelites were very broad in their interpretation, holding "some indecency" as anything offensive to the husband.⁹⁵ Rabbi Aqiba was a typical member of the Hillel School; he saw it acceptable to divorce a wife "even if he found another fairer than she."⁹⁶ To add fuel to the debate, the Qumran Community seems to have had even stricter laws about divorce than Shammai. They prohibited both polygamy and divorce; a man was not to marry as long as his spouse was living.⁹⁷

(a) Verses 3–8. The Pharisees seek to test Jesus' orthodoxy by asking him, "Is it lawful for a man to divorce his wife on every

---

90 So Eduard Schweizer, *The Good News According to Mark*, trans. Donald H. Madvig (Atlanta: John Knox Press, 1970), 201; R.A. Cole, *The Gospel According to St. Mark*, Tyndale NT Commentaries (Grand Rapids: Eerdmans, 1961), 158; Gould, 186.
91 F. Crawford Burkitt, *The Gospel History and Its Transmission*, 3rd ed. (Edinburgh: T. and T. Clark, 1911), 100–01.
92 A.T. Robertson, *Word Pictures in the New Testament* (Nashville, TN: Broadman Press, 1931), 1.350.
93 Mishnah Gittin ix.10.
94 David W. Amram, *The Jewish Law of Divorce According to the Bible and Talmud* (Philadelphia: Edward Stern, 1896), 33.
95 Amram, 33.
96 Mishnah Gittin, ix.10.
97 James R. Mueller, "The Temple Scroll and the Gospel Divorce Texts," *Revue de Qumran*, 10 (1979–81), 250–51. Cf. Harold S. Songer, "The Sermon on the Mount and Its Jewish Foreground," *Review and Expositor*, 89 (Spring 1992), 168–69.

ground?" (v. 3). in other words, "Do you side with Hillel, Shammai, or the Essenes?" Matthew's account, by its very arrangement, clearly shows the shape of a rabbinic debate.[98]

Jesus counters with his own question. His response, "Have you not read...?"(v. 4), would suggest that the Pharisees were well acquainted with what he is about to say, and that their desire to test him is not a genuine search for knowledge, but is malevolent.[99]

As in Mark, Jesus refers to the Genesis accounts of the first man and woman. Here, he appeals to the order of creation in Genesis 1:27, combining it with Genesis 2:24 as the divine initiative[100] of creating man and woman for each other and, in God's purposes, they are one body. Consequently, separation is unthinkable.[101]

The Pharisees undoubtedly understand the basis of Jesus' argument, but his statement that marriage should be indissoluble is totally against what they believe. Accordingly, they oppose his argument with another text, Deuteronomy 24:1. They believe that the text binds a man to divorce his wife for "some indecency."[102] And so they appeal to Moses, "Why then did Moses command that she be given a certificate of divorce and dismissed (*apolusai*)?" (v. 7).

Jesus' response is incisive. Moses did not command divorce. Rather, "on account of the hardness of your hearts he allowed you to divorce (*apolusai*) your wives" (v. 8). And he again stresses that such a toleration of an existing human institution is a departure from God's intention according to the created order[103] ("but from the beginning it was not so").

(b)*The "exception clause."* Verse 9 is the climactic point in Jesus' argument with the Pharisees. The use of the phrase, "And I tell you," is typical of Matthew when Jesus gives a divine revelation which supersedes the law of Moses.[104] Here, Jesus says succinctly that, apart from reasons of unchastity, the man who divorces his wife and

---

98 Daube, 72ff.
99 Gundry, 378.
100 There is some debate about "and he said". Gundry, 378 takes these words to refer to Jesus as the speaker. Albright and Mann, 226 assert that they are far more likely to refer to the Creator, the antecedent to v. 4. Dupont, 32 believes that Adam is the speaker.
101 Albright and Mann, 226.
102 Isaksson, 126. He argues, further, that when Mark (10:3,4) has Jesus ask, "What did Moses *command* you?" and the Pharisees answer, "Moses *allowed*...," Mark is diverging from reality. The verbs should be reversed. Matthew, trained rabbinically, was far more familiar with the viewpoint of the Pharisees, and thus was more original in his record than Mark (101–02). Cf. Shaner, 46–47.
103 Allen, 204.
104 Jack Dean Kingsbury, *Matthew: Structure, Christology, Kingdom* (Philadelphia: Fortress Press, 1975), 91.

marries another commits adultery; and the one who marries a divorced woman becomes an adulterer.

Matthew's inclusion of the exception, *me epi porneia*, "except for unchastity," here[105] has proved a stumbling block to many commentators. Why do the Matthean versions contain it while the others do not?

A common view with many scholars is that, apart from the exception clause, Matthew's saying is as close to the original saying of Jesus as one can get. In fact, Matthew probably borrowed it from Mark.[106] The exception clause, on the other hand, was added later to accommodate the realities of the community situation.[107] Other writers hold that the Matthean version is genuine in its entirety and the exception clause is a part of Jesus' teaching.[108]

Some have attempted to reconcile the differences between Matthew and the other versions by placing a different meaning on the exception clause from that traditionally accepted (i.e. the phrase, "except for unchastity"). One of the more common arguments is that the exception clause refers to an illicit union between persons of close kinship. Thus, Jesus was referring to a violation of the levitical incest laws.[109] But Jesus was talking about divorce, and a union which was not a genuine marriage would not require dissolution by divorce. Another suggestion is that the clause refers to premarital unchastity (Dt. 22:20–21).[110] If a husband were to discover that his wife had been unfaithful before marriage, in other words, he might divorce her. But there is no evidence that *porneia* was ever used in so narrow a fashion. One may well ask how unfaithfulness before a marriage could be more important than unfaithfulness during a marriage. Still another

---

[105] And in Mt. 5:32, where it is *parektos logou porneias*, "apart from a matter of unchastity"). For a more detailed discussion of the exception clause, see David Instone-Brewer, *Divorce and Remarriage in the Bible* (Grand Rapids: Eerdmans, 2002), 152–59.

[106] So Gundry, 381; Shaner, 47.

[107] So Alfred Plummer, *An Exegetical Commentary on the Gospel According to Saint Matthew* (London: Scott, 1928), 259f.

[108] So Stott, 17–18; Stanley A. Ellisen, *Divorce and Remarriage in the Church*, rev.ed. (Grand Rapids: Zondervan Press, 1980), 50–51; Aidan Mahoney, "A New Look at the Divorce Clauses in Mt. 5,32 and 19,9," *Catholic Biblical Quarterly*, 30 (1968), 29–30, and Phillip H. Wiebe, "Jesus' Divorce Exception," *Journal of the Evangelical Theological Society*, 32 (September 1989), 327–33. The most common argument of this view is that Mark and Luke simply assume that everyone knows that unchastity in marriage is adequate reason for divorce.

[109] Fitzmyer, 210. Cf. Augustine Stock, "Matthean Divorce Texts," *Biblical Theology Bulletin*, 8 (1978), 24–30. Cf. W.A. Heth and Gordon J. Wenham, *Jesus and Divorce, the Problem with the Evangelical Consensus* (Nashville, TN: Thos. Nelson, 1985), esp. ch. 6.

[110] Isaksson, 135–42. Cf. Wiebe, "Jesus' Divorce Exception," 327–33.

proposes the preteritive interpretation of Augustine, that the exception clauses are parenthetical to their respective contexts and really should read, "setting aside the matter of *porneia*, or, *porneia* is not involved."[111] It is difficult to see, though, how this rendition differs greatly from the literal reading, although it is noted that Augustine believed that Christ was emphasizing "the greater crime of divorce unjustified by the classic provocation."[112]

It would seem, then, that a study of the meaning of *porneia* in the context of the exception clause is vital. Kittel defines *porneia* as "extramarital intercourse on the part of the wife."[113] He has not gone far enough, for he shows that the earliest uses of the term (during the intertestamental period) can be rendered as "incest," "unnatural vice," and "sodomy.".[114] In a concentrated study, using not only the New Testament but also the Apocrypha and Qumran materials, Bruce Malina concludes that *porneia* means: "1)unlawful sexual intercourse; 2)specifically, sexual intercourse with a cultic or commercial prostitute; 3)unlawful conduct in general."[115] One may conclude, then, that *porneia* has to do with any type of illicit sexual relationship; it may involve sexual activity with other than one's spouse, incest, sodomy, bestiality, homosexuality, and so forth.

Thus, verse 9 would read, "And I tell you, that whoever divorces his wife, except for sexual unfaithfulness, and marries another, commits adultery; and he who marries a divorcee commits adultery."[116]

Verses 10–12. This passage, supplementary to the divorce

---

[111] Bruce Vawter, "The Divorce Clauses in Mt. 5,32 and 19,9," *Catholic Biblical Quarterly*, 16 (1954), 162–63. It must be noted, however, that he has since retreated from this view (see Vawter, "Divorce and the New Testament," 535, n.13).
[112] Vawter, "The Divorce Clauses....." 163.
[113] F. Hauck and F. Schulz, *"porneia," Theological Dictionary of the New Testament*, 6.592.
[114] Hauck and Schulz, 587.
[115] Bruce Malina, "Does Porneia Mean Fornication?" *Novum Testamentum*, 14 (1972), 14–15. Cf. David Clyde Jones, "The Westminster Confession on Divorce and Remarriage," *Presbyterion: Covenant Seminary Review*, XVI (Spring 1990), 31–33. Cf. Craig Blomberg, "Marriage, Divorce, Remarriage, and Celibacy: An Exegesis of Matthew 19:3–12," *Trinity Journal*, 11NS (Fall 1990), 172–82.
[116] Given that Marcan priority is the best explanation of the Synoptic Problem, it is probable that the exception clause is a Matthean addition. Matthew, under the guidance of the Holy Spirit (just like Paul in I Cor. 7:10–16), gives Christians one situation where divorce is permissible. Regardless of whether one accepts such an explanation of the exception clause (or any other explanation), it is still an integral part of the text. There is no manuscript evidence that it is an interpolation or a later addition. Although attempts have been made in some texts to harmonize the two versions of the exception clause, none omit it. Since believers accept the canonical version as the inspired text, it must be accepted and dealt with.

teaching, is unique in the Gospels and is not easy to interpret. Some have suggested that it is a later insertion by an editor to reflect the community situation.[117] Others believe that there is no reason why this should not be seen as a genuine saying of Jesus.[118] And, indeed, we must see it as "the only available medium in which today's reader can receive the word of God."[119]

In verse 10, the disciples voice their objections to the absolutism of Jesus' teaching, declaring, "If the cause (*aitia*) (of divorce) between a man and woman is like that, then it is better not to marry." *Aitia* here no doubt refers back to verse 3. If there is no cause for divorce,[120] and if continued marriage is enjoined upon all, then it would be better to refrain from marriage completely.

Jesus' reply in verse 11 is, "All cannot accept this saying, but only those to whom it is given." One must ask whether Jesus is commenting on what the disciples have just said about marriage, or does he have in mind what he has just said about marriage and divorce? Several scholars choose the former and have Jesus commending celibacy, while admitting that not everyone can adhere to such a state.[121] But such a comment that not everyone will accept the disciples' notion that it would be better not to marry at all without the possibility of divorce, really seems rather trite.[122] Verses 3–9 and 10–12 must be understood as a whole; there is not therein one message concerning marriage and divorce, followed by a second on voluntary celibacy. It seems far more likely that Jesus is freely admitting that not everyone is capable of adhering to his teaching of lifelong marriage as expressed in verses 4–6. Hardheartedness is the natural human condition and it requires a special gift of God to remain together in a true oneness of flesh for a lifetime.

In verse 12, however, Jesus does commend voluntary celibacy under certain circumstances. Contrary to Mosaic Law, it may be God's will for some to remain "eunuchs for the sake of the kingdom

---

[117] So Allen, 204.
[118] So Schweizer, 383.
[119] Quentin Quesnell, "Made Themselves Eunuchs for the Kingdom of Heaven (Mt. 19,12)," *Catholic Biblical Quarterly*, 30 (1968), 338–40.
[120] Some commentators would have the disciples say, along with Allen, 204 that if divorce were restricted to unchastity, it would be better to be single, but Jesus' disciples surely would not have been astonished by the Shammaite school of thought.
[121] Allen, 205; Floyd V. Filson, *A Commentary on the Gospel According to St. Matthew*, Harper's NT Commentaries (New York: Harper and Row, 1960), 207.
[122] Francis W. Beare, *The Gospel According to Matthew, A Commentary* (Oxford: Basil Blackwell, 1981), 390.

of heaven."[123] Celibacy, like lifelong marriage, is a gift of God.[124] At the same time, Jesus does not demand that his followers be celibate. Marriage is a normal state for men and women. Therefore, "he who can accept this, let him accept it."

The Teaching of Paul

The essential teaching of Paul in regard to divorce and remarriage is found in 1 Corinthians 7:10–16. This passage is an integral part of Paul's comments on the place of sex in a Christian's life.[125]

The Corinthian Christians had written Paul, seeking clarification on certain issues that had caused dissension in their ranks. In 7:1, the Apostle makes reference to their letter and begins to answer it. Evidently, the problem underlying all their trouble was

...the belief, held apparently by a sizable number of Corinthians, that salvation has already been granted in its fullness. The Corinthians seem to have been ecstatics, convinced that they were gifted with a spirituality that in effect lifted them above the worldly and the physical.[126]

Two greatly different types of moral implications resulted from their conviction: (1) Some of them gave themselves over to licence, totally unconcerned with morality, for they held that the spirit is independent of, and unaffected by, the action of the body. (2) Others went in the opposite direction, becoming ascetics and denying their sexual urges,[127] even to the point of repudiating their spouses. It was to these two factions in particular that Paul addresses his remarks in chapter 7.

Divorce and believers: 7:7–11. In verses 10–11, Paul considers the matter of divorce between believers. Whereas earlier in this chapter, his words might be taken as advisory,[128] here he takes a very authoritative stance with the words, "I direct, not I, but the Lord." In other words, there can be no question about this matter; this teaching comes from Jesus himself.[129]

Paul does not often make specific references to the sayings of

---

[123] Schweizer, 383.
[124] The idea is that, while some men are born eunuchs and others have been made eunuchs for the purposes of society, some have figuratively become eunuchs by refusing to marry in order that they might better serve God.
[125] Victor Paul Furnish, *The Moral Teachings of Paul: Selected Issues* (Nashville, TN: Abingdon Press, 1979), 30.
[126] Furnish, 31.
[127] Furnish, 32.
[128] As in v. 6: "But this I say by way of concession, not of command."
[129] There is some debate as to whether Paul had access to the sayings of the historical Jesus, or if his direction were based upon charismatic insights [Peter Richardson, "'I Say, not the Lord': Personal Opinion, Apostolic Authority, and the

Jesus. There are two possibilities as to why he does so here: One is that Paul referred to the sayings whenever he could, but that he did not know many of them; this saying was one of those few he did know. The second possibility is that Paul knew much of what Jesus said, but quoted him only when he differed from the teachings of Judaism.[130] In this case, the divorce logia are at odds with both Hillel and Shammai in their interpretation of the Old Testament.[131]

There is another, more compelling reason as to why Paul cites Jesus here. It is more probable that the Apostle, facing a concrete situation, has already decided what he is going to say about divorce, and quotes this teaching of Jesus to bolster his position.[132]

The apostle's directive begins in an unusual way: "...the wife must not be separated (*choristhenai*) from her husband...." He deals with the wife before passing on to the husband (v. 11b): "...and the husband must not divorce (*aphienai*) his wife." One might expect Paul, a good Jew, to use the reverse order. But the suggestion is that Paul has a definite situation in mind. There are two lines of thinking on what that instance might be. Both may well have originated in ascetic views that saw conjugal activity as a hindrance to one's spiritual life, an unhappy chore. For example, a wife demands her conjugal rights and her husband, "in the first flush of ascetic enthusiasm (prepares) to divorce her," because her nagging is as much of a distraction as her passion.[133] Such a woman should not permit herself to be divorced from her husband. She should do

---

Development of Early Christian Halakah," *Tyndale Bulletin*, 31 (1980), 70]. James D.G. Dunn, "Prophetic 'I'sayings and the Jesus tradition: the importance of testing prophetic utterances within early Christianity," *New Testament Studies*, 24 (1977–78), 180 claims that v. 10 is a saying of the historical Jesus, part of the tradition accumulated by the early church. Certainly, it does seem to identify clearly with the divorce logia of the Synoptic Gospels. Others reject this view [e.g. Oscar Cullmann, *The Early Church*, ed. A.J.B. Higgins (London: SCM Press, 1956), 68ff.], noting that *Kurios* is generally used in the NT of the ascended Jesus, and that v. 10 points to the exalted Lord as the real source of Paul's teaching. Hans Conzelmann, *First Corinthians, Hermeneia* (Philadelphia: Fortress Press, 1975), 120 attempts to bridge the gap by declaring that the "regulation given by the historical Jesus is also that of the exalted Lord; it is a supernatural command."

130 C.K. Barrett, *Commentary on the First Epistle to the Corinthians*, Harper's NT Commentaries (New York: Harper and Row, 1968), 162. He prefers the second possibility.

131 Barrett, 162. He supposes that the exception clause is to be discounted as a real portion of Jesus' saying.

132 Jerome Murphy O'Connor, "The Divorced Woman in I Corinthians 7:10–11," *Journal of Biblical Literature*, 100 (1981), 601–06. Roger L. Omanson, "Interpreting Paul: Redemption, Not Legalism," *Christian Century*, 100 (May 11, 1983), 451–53 extends this argument to show that Paul was not legalistic but pastoral in his approach to the problems of the Corinthian church.

133 Murphy O'Connor, 604.

everything in her power to prevent a divorce from taking place. One may also go in the opposite direction, seeing a wife who wishes wholly to devote herself to the Lord, but who also has the impression that she is behaving in a profane and impure way by giving herself to her husband.[134] Thus, she leaves him to consecrate herself to the celibate life.

That the latter was far more likely (or, at least, that it is a case of a woman leaving her husband), is evidenced by Paul's interjection in verse 11: "...but if she has separated, let her remain unmarried"(*ean de kai choristhe, meneto agamos*). Even though *ean* is usually the particle of the most general eventuality, when it is combined with *kai* ("even" or "indeed"), it indicates an action which has already occurred.[135] It would seem, therefore, that Paul is referring to an already existing situation. The divorce was pending when he received visitors from Corinth with the news (1Cor. 1:11), and he writes presuming that the divorce is an accomplished fact.[136] Consequently, to keep matters from going from bad to worse, he admonishes that, if a divorce has indeed taken place, the wife is not to marry anyone else. Should she discover that she cannot live continently, her one recourse is reconciliation to her husband.

Some commentators have pointed out that Paul seems to be going against the clear teaching of the Lord.[137] Even before completing the directive he has made an exception! But Paul, like Moses, is only recognizing the hardness of the human heart, even among believers. "But if she has separated..." is an acceptance that one cannot always stick to the absolute. To accept ethical relativity does not mean that one must do away with the absolute moral demand.[138]

It may be noted in verse 11 that Paul does not give a similar directive to the husband who may divorce his wife. The flow of thought, nonetheless, would dictate that the same recognition is there, albeit unspoken.

One of the major problems here and throughout the passage touches on Paul's use of words to designate the separation of spouses. He uses *aphiemi* in verses 11, 12, and 13, but *chorizœ in verses 10, 11, and 15. Does he use them synonymously to denote divorce? Or is he*

---

[134] Gaston Deluz, *La Sagesse de Dieu, explication de la première épître aux Corinthiens* (Neuchatel: Editions Delachaux et Niestlé, 1959), 100.

[135] EB Allo, *StPaul: Première Epitre aux Corinthiens*, 2ieme ed. (Paris: Librarire Lecoffre, 1956), 163. Cf. Conzelmann, 120.

[136] David L. Dungan, *The Sayings of Jesus in the Churches of Paul* (Philadelphia: Fortress Press, 1971), 90.

[137] So Dungan, 90–91; Barrett, 162–63.

[138] H.G. Coiner, "Those 'Divorce and Remarriage Passages'," *Concordia Theological Monthly*, 39 (1968), 382.

deliberately making a distinction?

There is no question that *aphiemi* refers to divorce. While it can mean a number of things, its legal sense, used here, is "divorce."[139] There is, however, some question about *chorizœ*.

One vein of thought insists that a proper interpretation of this word in this passage would denote simple desertion.[140] It declares that *chorizœ* in the New Testament does not refer to legal divorce and makes a distinction in Mark 10 between the author's use of *chorizo* and *apoluo* (which corresponds to *aphiemi*).[141]

A similar approach is to suggest that Paul's use of two different words, "separate" for the wife (*chorizo*) and "divorce" for her husband (*aphiemi*), would possibly reflect his Hebrew background in which divorce was permitted only to the husband.[142] It may well involve "more than the refusal of conjugal rights, but less than legal divorce...."[143]

It is difficult to find such arguments convincing. Those who hold to such views seem to be reading back into the text some notion of our present-day legal separation. But it cannot be emphasized too strongly that the world of the New Testament time knew nothing of such a situation.

The Greek, *chorizo*, is often used of divorce in the papyri and elsewhere.[144] The verb should be properly rendered "divorce", for even though in the middle passive form it can occasionally mean "depart", this is hardly sufficient basis for translating *me choristhenai* as "let her depart".[145] In 1 Corinthians 7:10–11, *me choristhenai* (passive) and *me aphienai* (active) are no different in essential meaning; the former is well documented as a technical term for "divorce" and certainly has that meaning here.[146]

One may glean further evidence from the New Testament itself. In Matthew 19:6 and Mark 10:9, Jesus is obviously referring to divorce when, after quoting Genesis 2:24 as the basis for marriage, he concludes, "What God has yoked together, let no man separate

---

[139] Arndt and Gingrich, 125.
[140] J.K. Elliott, "Paul's Teaching on Marriage in I Corinthians: Some Problems Considered," *New Testament Studies*, 19 (1972–73), 224.
[141] Elliott, 224.
[142] Barrett, 162.
[143] Barrett, 166.
[144] M.J. Harris and Colin Brown, "Separate, Divide (*chorizo*), *New International Dictionary of New Testament Theology*, 3.154.
[145] Fitzmyer, 211.
[146] Murphy O'Connor, 605. Cf. James H. Moulton and George Milligan, *The Vocabulary of the Greek New Testament* (London: Hodder and Stoughton, 1949), 695 for further information.

(*anthropos me chorizeto*)." Moreover, one may well ask, if divorce is not in view in verses 10–11, why does Paul dictate that the woman who has been separated from her husband must remain *agamos* (unmarried or "demarried")? How can one who is still married (albeit separated) be *agamos*? It is evident that the two terms must be considered as synonymous in this context. Paul uses both to refer to the legal dissolution of marriage.

Divorce and the unequally yoked: 7:12–16. Having dealt with marriage breakdown between two professing Christians, Paul now turns "to the rest," those cases where one spouse is a believer and the other is not. It is probable that, with the evangelization of Corinth, situations had arisen among married couples where one partner had been converted, but not the other. The question would naturally have followed: "Is it proper for a believer to remain married to an unbeliever?"[147]

In responding, Paul notes (unlike v. 10): "I am speaking, not the Lord." The Apostle is touching upon a relationship with which Jesus had never been confronted. Consequently, his directive was his own. One must not, however, see his statement as private opinion. On the contrary, his teaching is given all the inspiration and authority of an Apostle.[148] He speaks as one who has the mind of Christ.

(a) The viable mixed marriage (7:12–14). Paul's advice is straightforward: if a Christian husband has an unbelieving wife who is content to live with him, he should not divorce her; and if a Christian woman has an unbelieving husband who is content to live with her, she should not divorce him. The use of *suneudokei* ("content") suggests a mutual consent, indicating that both husband and wife find the situation agreeable.[149] What the Apostle is saying, in essence, is: If the unbelieving spouse does not want a divorce, and if the marriage is mutually satisfying, the believer is not to ask for a divorce.

Paul's instruction here is in contrast to the teaching of the Old Testament. The Hebrews had been instructed to keep away from heathen partners. Indeed, Ezra (10:11) and Nehemiah (13:23,24) condemned mixed marriages, and the former instructed God's people to divorce heathen spouses. While Paul does not permit marriages between believers and unbelievers (see 2 Cor. 6:14–15),

---

[147]. Carl Laney, "Paul and the Permanence of Marriage in I Corinthians 7," *Journal of the Evangelical Theological Society*, 25 (Sept. 1982), 286.
[148] Archibald Robertson and Alfred Plummer, *The First Epistle of Paul to the Corinthians*, International Critical Commentary (Edinburgh: T. and T. Clark, 1911), 141.
[149] Robertson and Plummer, 141.

neither does he seek the dissolution of existing marriages. In fact, he reminds his readers that the pagan partner is consecrated (*hegiasti*) through the believer. As to just what is meant here is unclear, and attempts to explain what Paul is saying are far from satisfying. One commentator dwells upon the passive nature of the verb in its combination with *en te gunaiki* ("in connection with the wife") to note that a certain passive sanctity is bestowed upon the pagan partner when he is joined by marriage to a believing spouse.[150] Just how that sanctifying takes place he does not say. Another sees this holiness as an outward thing, conferred by sexual intercourse with the Christian partner.[151] Still another declares that it is the unbeliever's persistence to persevere in union with his believing wife that makes him acceptable to God, for in such a manner he is participating with her, to a degree, in the Christian way.[152] In verse 14, Paul argues that these marriages must have consecrated parents, "otherwise your children are unclean," which is not the case. It may well be that Paul is thinking in Jewish patterns: "The children are within the covenant; this could not be so if the marriage itself were unclean."[153]

(b) *The unviable mixed marriage (7:15–16).* In many mixed marriages, undoubtedly there was harmony. But in others, the conversion of husband or wife had evidently caused discord. Consequently, Paul gives a final directive: If the unbelieving spouse wishes to separate, *chorizesthœ*, "let him separate" (or, "divorce"). In other words, if the unbelieving spouse clearly demonstrates that he or she wants the marriage ended, the believer should not stand in the way.[154] The continuance or dissolution of the marriage is based on the last part of verse 15: "...but God has called you to peace." Paul realizes that the quality of a marriage is of vital concern; when mutual love and respect have vanished, the marriage may be dissolved.[155] God does not call Christians to maintain a marriage of pressure and dissension with a partner who is committed neither to Jesus Christ nor to the marriage.[156]

---

[150] R.C.H. Lenski, *The Interpretation of St. Paul's First and Second Epistles to the Corinthians* (Columbus, OH: Wartburg Press, 1946), 292.
[151] John E. McFayden, *The Epistles to the Corinthians and Galatians* (New York: A.S. Barnes, 1909), 46. Cf. Calvin, *Corinthians*, 241.
[152] Frederic L. Godet, *Commentary on First Corinthians* (1889; rpt. Grand Rapids: Kregel, 1977), 340.
[153] Barrett, 165. Contrary to the belief of some, Paul cannot be referring here to infant baptism, for to do so would mean that a child was not *hegiasti* at birth.
[154] Adams, 47.
[155] Furnish, 45–46.
[156] Robert G. Bratcher, *A Translator's Guide to Paul's First Letter to the Corinthians* (London: United Bible Societies, 1982), 61.

In cases where the unbeliever gets a divorce, Paul says that the believer is "not bound" (*ou dedoulotai*). What does he mean? To what (or, to what degree) is the believing spouse not bound?

There are those who see the meaning of this phrase as signifying that the believing spouse is not under obligation to engage in all sorts of legal manoeuvres to continue the marriage. At the same time, remarriage cannot be allowed: "Paul is saying in 1 Corinthians 7 that the marriage relationship is binding until death (v. 39), but a rejected spouse is not 'enslaved' to the extent of having to maintain the marriage...."[157] Others take verse 15 to allow another marriage: "...the Christian is not subjected to any constraint because of the pagan's behaviour. He can marry again."[158]

This latter stance seems more reasonable than the former. If the believer is free to permit divorce but not free to remarry, then he is not really free at all. He is still under bondage to the unbeliever. But the believing spouse is, in fact, set free by the unbeliever's action; that freedom is all inclusive.

There has been debate, as well, as to the meaning of verse 16: *ti gar oidas ei*, etc. "...for how do you know, etc...?" What does Paul mean? With *ei* following *oidas*, the syntax allows an argument either against the believer's accepting divorce, or in favour of so doing.[159] Paul may be saying, "Do not fight divorce in the hope that, if you remain, you may convert your spouse," or he may be saying (by connecting the statement with *me aphieto* in vv. 13 and 14), "Try to avoid a divorce because it is possible that you may convert your partner."[160] The former is better suited to the context, for the latter would necessitate *ei* being understood in the sense of *ei me* (which is not in the text!).[161] Should the unbeliever insist upon a divorce, it should be granted for the sake of peace, because there is no assurance that this spouse will be saved if the marriage continues.[162]

Conclusions

When one turns to the New Testament, one comes to the core of the divorce and remarriage dilemma in the teachings of Jesus. Each of the Synoptic writers quotes the Lord on divorce and remarriage.

---

[157] Laney, 287–88. Cf. Dungan, 97 and Coiner, 383.
[158] Conzelmann, 123. Cf. Atkinson, 124 and Morris, 111.
[159] Robertson, *Word Pictures*, 6.128–29.
[160] Robertson and Plummer, 144.
[161] For a good overview of the pros and cons of this problem, see Conzelmann, 124, n. 47–48. Cf. Gordon D. Fee, "I Corinthians vii.16: Optimistic or Pessimistic?" *New Testament Studies*, 24 (1977–78), 539–44.
[162] Laney, 289.

Mark 10:11–12 and Luke 16:18 are virtually identical, saying essentially: "Everyone divorcing his wife and marrying another commits adultery, and he who marries a divorcee commits adultery." Matthew is not unlike the others, save for his "exception clause", which permits divorce on the ground of sexual unfaithfulness.

Jesus' teaching is hard to receive, especially if one holds that he did not ever make an exception. How can one reconcile his teaching with reality?

It must be remembered that this teaching (especially Mt. 5:31,32) is illustrative of the Kingdom of God, a period yet to come, which will be the perfect fulfillment of the Law and the Divine intention.[163] This teaching on divorce and remarriage is no easier nor more difficult to practice than the other teachings concerning Kingdom living. Moreover, it would seem that Jesus, as he often does elsewhere, here overstates his case in order to demonstrate how completely contrary divorce is to the Divine intention for man and woman. That he does so may be seen by the fact that both Matthew and Paul feel compelled to make exceptions.[164]

In the context of Matthew 19, verse 12 is often overlooked. Jesus' teaching, "He who is able to receive it (i.e. his teaching), let him receive it," is a new interpretation of marriage and singleness. It brings a new vision of God's will and especially of the worth of womankind. It is an insight far in advance of Jesus' time.[165]

The Apostle Paul uses Jesus' saying as the foundation for his own teaching, but combines it with original comments. He prohibits divorce between believers, but then admits exceptions to Jesus' teaching. If a believer is adamant about divorcing a believing spouse, that is permissible, providing the one separating remains unmarried.

In dealing with marriage issues with which Jesus was never faced, Paul makes another exception. If a mixed marriage is mutually satisfying, a believer should remain married to a pagan spouse. On the other hand, if the unbeliever insists upon a divorce, the believing spouse, for the sake of peace, should not stand in the way.

It is probable that Paul's teaching in 1Corinthians 7 is sapiential (wisdom) in nature.[166] He is not dealing with abstractions, but with *de facto* conditions. Consequently, he bolsters what he has to say with

---

[163] Dwight Hervey Small, *The Right to Remarry* (Westwood, NJ: Fleming H. Revell, 1976), 44–45.
[164] Stein, 119.
[165] R. Lofton Hudson, *'Til Divorce Do Us Part* (Nashville, TN: Thos. Nelson, 1974), 47.
[166] James A. Fischer, "I Cor. 7:8–24 — Marriage and Divorce," *Biblical Research*, 23 (1978), 24. For a more comprehensive consideration of Paul as "wise man", see Fischer, "Pauline Literary Forms and Thought Patterns," *Catholic Biblical Quarterly*, 39 (1977), 209–23. Richardson, 84–86 advances the idea that Paul is not

Jesus' saying, but also seeks to give deeper insights as to how a Christian may best reflect the image of God and devote himself/herself to spiritual pursuits in peace and harmony.[167]

Paul's exceptions make it clear that neither Jesus' sayings nor his own directives should be seen as "Christian casuistry" (law). Paul is not a legislator setting forth a new decree on divorce, but a wise counsellor seeking to guide his flock.[168] We must conclude that the Apostle sees his instruction "not as a binding precept, but as a significant directive whose relevance to a particular situation has to be evaluated by the pastor responsible for the community."[169]

---

developing his own *halakah*, but admits that his thesis is not firmly established.
[167] Fischer, "I Cor. 7…," 34–35.
[168] Coiner, 384.
[169] Murphy O'Connor, 606. Cf. Blomberg, 195–96 for a fine summary of the NT view of divorce and remarriage.

Chapter 5

Moral Aspects of Divorce and Remarriage

The critical examination of the major passages dealing with divorce and remarriage has shown that, while divorce militates against God's intention for husbands and wives, he does not always condemn it in and of itself. In fact, there have been times when God himself initiated or commanded divorce proceedings.

In view of what the Bible says about the problem, and because the canon of Scripture has always been accepted as the premier guidepost of the church, Christians have an obligation to examine carefully the morality of divorce and remarriage. To do so in the light of what Scripture says is doubly important because most, if not all, believers have the tendency to start with a particular theological or moral outlook and attempt to find biblical support for their own views, rather than to begin with the Bible and formulate their theology and ethical standards from what it has to say.

Arguments Explicit in Scripture

A number of issues in regard to the morality of divorce and remarriage are easy to determine because the Bible explicitly sets them forth.

Sexual infidelity. That divorce is permitted where a spouse is guilty of sexual unfaithfulness is clear from an examination of both the Old Testament and Matthean records of Jesus' teaching. One must make a distinction between sexual infidelity (*porneia*) and adultery (*moicheia*): the former refers to sexual sins of any and every kind, whereas adultery is that which breaks faith with one's marriage partner, a violation of the marriage covenant.[1] *Porneia* does not involve only sexual intercourse. Just cause for divorce would also include such sins as incest, pedophilia, bestiality, addiction to pornography, and homosexuality.

It has been shown that the basis of true marriage is *troth*, or faithfulness. A particular man and a particular woman respond to

---

1 H. Reisser, "*moicheuo*," *New International Dictionary of New Testament Theology*, 2. 582–84. Cf. Jay E. Adams, *Marriage, Divorce, and Remarriage in the Bible* (Grand Rapids: Baker Book House, 1980), 54–55.

God's call to become one flesh and thus to participate in His creative activity. The initial sign of this contracting together is, normally, the physical consummation of the union. Just as the couple become one flesh in the physical sense, so they become one flesh in every other sense as well. "Upon love alone the validity of intercourse and the permanence of marriage depend, and love means nothing if not fully-willed, unqualified fidelity."[2]

Sexual infidelity wreaks havoc with the one-flesh concept as it simultaneously destroys the commitment to faithfulness. It is a defiant rejection of the covenant to "love, honour, and cherish", along with God's will that declares the permanency of marriage. It was because of Israel's flagrant and continued breaches of her commitment of faithfulness to God that he divorced her and threatened to do the same to Judah.

Throughout the Bible, sexual perversity is condemned as a crime of great enormity. Indeed, among the Jews of the latter biblical era, it was regarded in such a grave light that a Jew whose wife had committed such a transgression was obliged to divorce her; there was no option.[3] It is small wonder, then, that Matthew gives to Jesus' teaching the exception for sexual unfaithfulness.

One may go even further and say that it is sinful to continue in a marriage under such conditions. One commentator has put it well: "If one's partner is playing the harlot or tomcat with someone else, it is more of a sin to continue to lie with that one than to separate. To be submissive under such an arrangement by condoning it is to be a party to it."[4] Divorce in such a situation is almost mandatory.

At the same time, one must realize that it is God's desire, first and foremost, that reconciliation be effected wherever possible. Though divorce is permissible, a spouse may forgive the transgressor if he/she repents. Hosea is exemplary of the proper attitude of godly love. Jesus commands, furthermore, "If your brother (and it applies equally to one's spouse) sins, rebuke him; and if he repents, forgive him" (Lk. 17:3). In such a situation, faithfulness must be pledged anew and a fresh relationship begun.

Should reconciliation fail and divorce proceed, is remarriage possible or permissible for the "innocent" spouse? The Old Testament assumes that remarriage will occur in the event of a divorce (indeed, the ancient Hebrew divorce certificate noted that

---

2 Derrick Sherwin Bailey, *The Mystery of Love and Marriage, A Study of the Theology of Sexual Relation* (New York: Harper and Bros., 1952), 79.
3 *Mishnah Kethuboth* iii.4–5.
4 Stanley R. Ellisen, *Divorce and Remarriage in the Church*, rev.ed. (Grand Rapids: Zondervan, 1980), 54.

the divorced spouse was free to remarry). Matthew assumes that remarriage will occur in the event of a divorce on the ground of sexual infidelity. He recognizes that such a heinous sin has destroyed the first union. Without such a ground, the second marriage is adulterous. But here a new union may be contracted and recognized by God.

What about the transgressing spouse? There is no question that sexual infidelity is a great wrong. And as long as one remains in such a state, no church should either solemnize or recognize a second marriage. At the same time, the grace of God is efficacious for the worst of sins (Rom. 5:20). If a transgressor repents, then the sin, being forgiven, should be remembered no more (Isa. 44:22).[5] Repentance opens the door to remarriage (certainly, it should be ascertained as closely as possible that the repentance is genuine). The first step, properly, is the seeking of reconciliation with the former spouse or, if reconciliation is not possible, that person's forgiveness. If the former spouse refuses to be reconciled or has already married another, then the door is open to remarriage for the former transgressor.

That there is ample biblical precedent for such a stand is seen in the Old Testament account of David and Bathsheba (II Sam. 11, 12). Both were guilty of adultery. Yet, upon their repentance, God forgave them and blessed their marriage. If this marriage, effected in the most grievous and sinful condition possible, could be accepted and even blessed by God, then there is no way that anyone can truthfully claim that God will refuse to allow and bless the marriage of another penitent adulterer.

Spiritual separation. Mixed marriages (i.e. believer to unbeliever) have always posed a problem for the church. These marriages may be placed in three categories: (1) where a believer has married an unbeliever, such marriages were prohibited by the Apostle Paul who commanded that Christians should marry "only in the Lord" (I Cor. 7:40);[6] (2) where, at the time of the marriage, both were unbelievers, but one of the spouses was later converted to Christ; and (3) where, at the time of the marriage, both were believers, but one of the spouses later rejected his/her commitment to Christ.

Paul's teaching on the subject has been accurately presented. If the marriage is mutually satisfying and the unbeliever does not wish

---

[5] If the penitent was unsaved at the time of the sin and has since come to Christ, then 2 Cor. 5:17 is applicable: He/she is a "new creation" in Christ.
[6] While this particular injunction is addressed (in its context) to widows, it accurately represents the Apostle's position for all believers. Cf. 2 Cor. 6:14. The church has an obligation to refuse to solemnize such marriages, although once they occur, it cannot refuse to minister to both spouses.

to secure a divorce, then the union should persist. If the unbeliever desires the dissolution of the marriage, it should be granted.

One further argument should be noted. Continued attempts by the unbeliever to hinder, restrain, or prevent the believer from exercising his/her faith may be construed as ground for divorce.

Much has been written by conservative Christians about the necessity of a wife's submission to her husband. Many of these suggest that the Bible commands submission without qualification.[7] Some go so far as to declare that a wife is to obey her husband even if such obedience involves her participation in sin.[8] Such a pernicious view is destructive to marriage in general and to womanhood in particular. No woman need feel that she must remain with a man who attempts to force her to reject her faith or to be a participant in degrading activities.

Luther notes, and rightly so, that "if the non-Christian should not let his spouse be a Christian and should hinder and persecute him, then it would be time to keep these words of Christ also physically: 'He who loves wife or child more than Me is not worthy of Me' (Mt. 10:37)."[9] Divorce in such a case is permissible, for a higher law is in effect, the law of duty to God above all else. In further commenting on this cause, Luther quotes Deuteronomy 13:6ff., in which God's people are commanded to put to death anyone, even a wife or child, if that person advocates turning away from God. "But in the New Testament, where one does not kill the body, it is sufficient to divorce."[10]

As always, there should be an attempt on the part of the believer to be reconciled, conditional on the unbeliever's change in attitude. If, however, after a reasonable time, no reconciliation can be effected, then "the brother or sister is not bound" (I Cor. 7:15). Remarriage is appropriate.

Desertion. Desertion of a spouse is another cause that would fall under Paul's directive in 1Corinthians 7:12–16.[11] There are few ways of saying more clearly that the dissolution of the marriage is desired.

---

7 As Larry Christenson, *The Christian Family* (Minneapolis: Bethany Fellowship, 1970), 41. Cf. Mirabel Morgan, *The Total Woman* (Old Tappan, NJ: Fleming H. Revell, 1973), 71.
8 So Darien Cooper, *You Can Be the Wife of a Happy Husband* (Wheaton, IL: Victor Books, 1974), 71.
9 Martin Luther, "Commentaries on 1 Corinthians 7," *Luther's Works*, ed. Hilton C. Oswald (St. Louis: Concordia Press, 1973), 28:19.
10 Luther, 34.
11 Any professing believer who would desert spouse and/or family would be acting no differently from an unbeliever and, to all intents and purposes, should be seen in a similar light.

It must be realized, furthermore, that the abandonment of one's spouse and offspring may often be more vicious and deadly than sexual unfaithfulness. It often leaves the spouse in a bewildering and uncertain predicament. Does the deserting spouse intend the dissolution of the marriage? What lies behind such an action? Will the deserter ever return? If so, when? What should be the reaction of the one abandoned?

Desertion, like sexual perversity, fractures one's commitment to fidelity. Often, the reason for the desertion is some sexual unfaithfulness. At any rate, the transgressing spouse is no longer a "help meet" for his/her partner, and the oneness of flesh, the conjugal community willed by God, has been torn asunder.

Such a case should be treated in precisely the same way as sexual infidelity. The offending spouse has, by the action taken, both displayed unfaithfulness and demanded the dissolution of the marriage. The other partner is not bound. There is no obligation to wait for the former to return (for who knows even if he/she will return?) in order to attempt reconciliation, but the spouse is free. If another marriage is desired, well and good.

Arguments Inferred from Scripture

Not all moral aspects of divorce and remarriage are explicitly set forth in the Scriptures. Some are there by analogy or inference. There is biblical support for them, but they must be brought forth as gold from a mine, unearthed, excavated, and polished. That more toil is required to set them out does not make them any the less valid or precious.

Irreconcilable differences. Acts 15:36ff. records a dispute between Paul and Barnabas concerning a proposed return missionary tour of Pamphylia. On the first trip, John Mark had accompanied them, but he had abandoned the work halfway through to return home. Barnabas wanted to give the young man another chance, but Paul refused. The writer notes that "there was such a sharp feeling that they separated (*apochœristh~nai*) from each other" (15:39a).[12] Here were two men of full Christian maturity, exemplars of the faith, who, in spite of Jesus' teachings on reconciliation and humility, had such sharp differences of opinion that they were unable to be reconciled but had to go their separate ways.

Cannot the same problem occur within marriage? A man and

---

12 It is noteworthy that *apochoristhenai*, "to separate completely", comes from *chorizo*, which Paul uses in 1 Cor. 7 for "divorce".

wife, both believers, come to hold such sharp and differing opinions that mutual love, respect, and submission are shattered. They cannot seem to find any common ground, even with extensive counselling. The only recourse seems to be to go their separate ways.

The account in Acts does not excuse such behaviour any more than it excuses the behaviour of Paul and Barnabas. It does, however, provide some insight into what can happen. Sometimes, irreconcilable differences necessitate divorce, even when such a course of action is sinful.

The New Testament reason given for exceptional divorce is hardness of heart. Such a state has been defined as "the *de facto* condition of man between the Fall and the Last Judgment."[13] It has been argued that, when God allowed the Jews to divorce, he was acting kindly and wisely. Jesus presumed, in his teachings, that his followers had overcome that hard-heartedness through being spiritually reborn. But it is evident that Christians still suffer no less than the ancient Jews from that same malady. Is it not better, then, to divorce rather than continue to quarrel, slander, and persecute each other?[14] One may infer from the Bible that, given human obduracy, sometimes divorce is necessary when differences cannot be reconciled.

Paul and Barnabas separated. And, in spite of the origin of their separation in sinful hardness of heart, God used it to bring forth greater good (there were now two missionary teams rather than one). Why cannot God likewise take sinful, stubborn divorced persons and bring good out of bad for his purposes?

The lesser of evils. Sometimes, when problems arise in the course of a marriage, there seem to be no solutions that are not sinful. In such cases, one may be obliged to pursue a course which is discerned as the lesser of evils. For example, a woman is married to a man who abuses her and their children both verbally and physically. There is no specific biblical injunction given for divorce under such circumstances. Nor is it right for the woman to allow herself and her children to be persecuted. There is no "right" way out. In such a case, one must ask whether it is better to endure abuse or seek a divorce.

In seeking counsel from the Bible, it is evident that the husband in the above example has ignored Jesus' command to "love your neighbour as yourself" (Mt. 22:39), and has destroyed the mutual love and respect demanded in marriage by the pledge of troth. To remain with such a man would, further, expose the family to physical

---

13 Helmut Thielicke, *Theological Ethics*, trans. John W. Doberstein (Grand Rapids: Eerdmans, 1981), III, 66.
14 Robert Kehl, "Ehescheidung, ja oder nein?" *Reformatio*, 14 (July 1965), 385–86.

and possible emotional breakdown. It would seem that the lesser of evils would clearly be to cut oneself off completely from such a spouse and dissolve so ruinous a union.

To take such a course of action does not mean that the separating spouse should totally ignore the offender. Christian love demands the seeking of reconciliation for a reasonable length of time and, if necessary, a unilateral forgiveness of the offender by the offended. At the same time, unilateral forgiveness does not mean that the victimized spouse must return to the victimizer. That would depend on the continuing attitude and behaviour of the victimizer.

Better to Marry than to Burn

It has been shown that divorce is a departure from God's ideal, which is the lifelong unity of one particular man and one particular woman. Because divorce falls short of the divine intention, it is not easy to consider remarriage, for the Bible does not commend sub-ideal behaviour. Nonetheless, it must be recognized that God, while he does not suggest lower ideals for his people, may permit them to operate on a sub-ideal level because of the fact of human sin.[15]

It has been demonstrated that remarriage following a divorce on the grounds of sexual unfaithfulness, spiritual separation, and desertion is permissible. The Old Testament assumes remarriage after divorce, and the Apostle Paul declares that the partner who has been injured "is not bound". For the church to legislate against remarriage in such cases (as does the Church of Rome) is to go against the Bible's teaching.[16]

The teachings of Jesus indicate that remarriage (other than for the grounds given above) constitutes adultery. There is no question of that. But it is at this point that the grace of God comes into operation. It may be asserted that the Gospel divorce sayings are principial in nature and not prescriptive; the same Jesus who laid down these ideals also forgave the woman at the well of Sychar who had had five husbands and was living common-law with a sixth (Jn. 4), and the woman taken in adultery (Jn. 8). Can and does he still not do the same?

If one sees adultery as a violation of the marriage covenant between the original spouses, then it becomes clear that, while remarriage does involve adultery, it relates only to the act whereby

---

15 George Peters, "What God Says About Remarriage," *Moody Monthly*, 78 (July 1978), 43.
16 Peters, 43.

the new marriage is initiated rather than to the marriage as a whole. Larry Richards acknowledges that

> The physical consummation of the new marriage may technically and in reality be an adulterous act. In such cases, it must be acknowledged as sin and dealt with as sin. It must be brought to the Lord in confession, expecting him to keep his promise to forgive and cleanse.[17]

There is an option for the divorced believer that should be examined before remarriage is considered. In 1Corinthians 7:32–34, Paul commends the celibate life as a means of effective Christian service. Marriage, because of the responsibility it entails, divides one's heart, while celibacy permits one to devote oneself to Christ. The divorced Christian should carefully question whether God may not be using such a predicament to call him/her to a selfless commitment to him.

Many Christians who have been previously married find continence a virtually impossible task. Once a sexual desire has been awakened and indulged, it is not easily subdued. The deprivation of marital commitment can lead to temptation and sin. One sampling of divorced Christians, for example, showed that only 9% of the men and 27% of the women were celibate even though 57% of the men and 55% of the women were regular church-goers, all of whom identified themselves as "born again."[18]

Emil Brunner proposes that a definition of marriage is needed that includes marriage as a *remedium concupiscentiae*[19] (remedy for concupiscence, or lust). In so doing, he is simply reiterating Paul's position: "It is better to marry than to burn" (1Cor. 7:9). Why cannot such a statement be applied to the divorced? It is! That is the context of Paul's advice. He is addressing "the *agamos* and the widows" (7:6). While it is often used to denote simply the "unmarried," *agamos* may also mean the "demarried."[20]

Surely, remarriage is better than promiscuity. There is considerable difference between technical adultery (i.e. remarriage following an illicit divorce) and continuing fornication. While the Bible clearly identifies remarriage following an illegitimate divorce as

---

17 Larry Richards, *Remarriage, A Healing Gift from God* (Waco, TX: Word Books, 1981), 69–70.
18 Harold Ivan Smith, "Sex and Singleness the Second Time Around," *Christianity Today*, 23 (May 25, 1979), 18.
19 Emil Brunner, *The Divine Imperative*, trans. Olive Wyon (Philadelphia: Westminster Press, 1947), 351.
20 David E. Garland, "The Christian's Posture Towards Marriage and Celibacy: I Corinthians 7," *Review and Expositor*, 80 (Summer 1980), 354. Cf. William F. Orr and James A. Walther, *I Corinthians, Anchor Bible* (Garden City, NY: Doubleday, 1976), 210.

sin, it does not deny forgiveness to the sinners involved should they repent, nor does it demand the abandonment of the second marriage.[21]

Paul demonstrates great wisdom and compassion in this matter in 1 Corinthians 7:26–28:

> I think then that it is good in view of the impending distress for a man to be so: Are you bound to a wife? Do not seek to be loosed (*lusin*). Have you been loosed *lelusai*) from a wife? Do not seek a wife. But if you have (*ean de kai*)[22] married, you have not sinned...

The Greek, *lusin*, "to be loosed," is one of the words for "divorced."[23] Paul may well be saying that the man who is divorced and remarried has not sinned. While the divorced woman is not explicitly mentioned, the flow of thought would tend to apply to her as well.

Conclusions

The purpose of divorce in the Old Testament was always for the purpose of remarriage. Since Jesus qualifies divorce (and so does Paul), then we may say that the purpose of divorce in the New Testament *may* be for remarriage.[24] As we have seen, above, there are good reasons for divorce explicitly set out in the Bible. These include infidelity, spiritual separation, and abandonment. But still other factors are inferred in Scripture, such as irreconcilable differences (even after extensive counselling), when divorce and remarriage is less of an evil than staying married to the original spouse, or, in the case of one already divorced, as a preventive for promiscuity.

---

21 Peters, 44.
22 See previous chapter, n.136, on the significance of *ean de kai*.
23 Many commentators would argue that these verses apply to the widowed, but there are no grounds for restricting them to that group alone. At the very least, they must be applied generally to all formerly married.
24 Craig Keener, "Free to Remarry," *Christianity Today*, 36 (14 December 1992), 34.

Chapter 6

Practical Implications

It does little good to do a detailed examination of what the Bible has to say about any given subject if one is not prepared to go farther and, from the exegesis, draw out practical applications for the present. The chief purpose of theology is to interact with the biblical materials to chart a fitting course of contemporary Christian action.

The task of this chapter is to derive from the previous exegesis of the divorce and remarriage passages some practical theological implications for today's church. Hopefully, these implications will be sufficiently pointed that others may use them to define specific practical programs to help alleviate this problem.

Implications for the Whole Community of Faith

If the church is to be the redemptive community that Christ has intended, then it must impart the Good News of hope to all, including the divorced. It must have an effective ministry both in marriage and its termination.

An ounce of prevention. While the church has an obligation to minister to those suffering marriage breakdown, it is far better served by seeking to impede the failure of marriages. This is especially true, given that a 1996 United Nations survey on divorce showed that the United States has the highest divorce rate in the world at 4.3 per 1,000 population; Canada was not far behind at 2.6.[1] Undoubtedly, the best way to do so is by strengthening marriage. There are various courses of action open to the achieving of this goal.

First, the church must proclaim God's intention for marriage. The whole basis of lifelong union is rooted in the Bible. Without the Genesis pictures of marriage and Jesus' affirmation of them, it is difficult to make a compelling case for one man and one woman remaining together until parted by death.

Most people, including professing Christians, do not think of marriage as a sacred institution ordained by God in which husband and wife become a new and distinct entity totally differentiated from all other human relational unities,[2] but rather as a stable living

---

[1] See website www.vifamily.ca/library/cft/divorce-htm/Canadian, June 22, 2004.
[2] Derrick Sherwin Bailey, *The Mystery of Love and Marriage, A Study in the Theology of Sexual Relations* (New York: Harper and Bros., 1952), 44.

arrangement for two individuals who find each other attractive. Marriage often becomes not a total fusion of husband and wife, but a simple co-existence of two persons of opposite sex who enter a convenient partnership of mutual interest and affection, which may at any time be broken should these interests cease to be mutual.[3]

Two reasons lie behind the failure to understand properly the true purposes of marriage: either people reject the basis of marriage set out in Christian theology or they are ignorant of it. In either case, the church must confront them with the biblical teaching. This message must be publicized not just within the walls of the church building, but throughout society as a whole.

Such a proclamation must include a recognition of the realism of the Bible in its assessment of human capability for achieving God's intention for marriage.[4] Nowhere does the Bible hold up an impossible standard which man must reach or else. in the Old Testament, because of sin in the human heart, God through Moses permitted divorce. Jesus' saying demonstrated the same acceptance of reality. He stressed the divine ideal of indissolubility, but also noted that "not all can accept this word" (Mt. 19:11). Paul, likewise, emphasized indissolubility, but gave several exceptions to the principle.

The church must emphasize that God does not expect people to be perfect. Of course, the ideal goal is there, but sin causes human beings to fall short of the mark. God knows and accepts that fact. Because he does, he will help fallible human beings to make the best of a bad job.

Again, there is a need for adequate marriage preparation. Since so many marriages are breaking down, it should stand to reason that many people have not been adequately trained for the realities of marriage.[5] The church has an obligation to provide opportunities for marriage preparedness. These opportunities should be afforded at every age level, beginning with sex education for children and extending beyond the wedding ceremony into marriage itself.

In an age where sex has become a commonplace commodity, the church must inform young people of the Christian view of sex in the service of relationship, rich and rewarding when used properly in

---

3 Mary Stewart Van Leeuwen, "Deconstructing the Culture of Divorce," *Christian Century*, 30 July—6 August 1997, 691.
4 Myrna and Robert Kysar, *The Asundered, Biblical Teaching on Divorce and Remarriage* (Atlanta: John Knox Press, 1980), 86.
5 Stanley L. Vugteveen, "Premarital Counseling: Helpful Suggestions for the Busy Pastor," *Reformed Review*, 35 (Winter 1982), 83 cites studies to show that 66% of divorced persons had received no premarital counselling.

the human encounter, destructive when abused.[6] At the marriage age, the church must stress the biblical view of marriage, particularly the need for commitment to the institution of marriage, and commitment on the part of each spouse to the other.[7] There must be opportunity for frank discussion of what such commitment entails: of the needs, ideals, goals, and attitudes of the other partner and how each can grow towards the other without losing individuality.

Continuing care is needed from the honeymoon on. The first few years are particularly important. "Like the perfection of any gift, marriage needs to be consistently practiced by those claiming the gift, and nurtured by those given an understanding of the gift's meaning and purpose."[8] Latter years are also fraught with danger, and care must be maintained. There are other pressure points which couples need to understand, such as the "empty-nest" period when, if there is not an on-going commitment to each other, spousal relationships may fracture.

Underlying all of this preparation is the need for a right relationship of spouses and their marriage to Jesus Christ. It is vital for the church to seize the initiative in guiding couples to bring their relationship into the proper order of spiritual priorities: Christ first, spouse second, and self last. Only then can they move towards marriage as the lifelong unity God intended it to be.

Amidst all that the church does in regard to marriage preparation, it should also be preparing young people for a life that may be single. The church — and this includes, pastors, other church leaders, and parents — must proclaim the viability of singleness. Not everyone should marry. Children should grow up being apprised of the fact that God calls some people to be single, and there is nothing wrong nor abnormal with such a state. It should be acknowledged that there are some things that one will never be able to do if one is married. There are some areas of Christian mission, for example, which are rendered impossible by marriage. Single people have far more time to put into spiritual preparation, devotion, and prayer than do married people. It is admirable to be single "for the sake of the kingdom of God" (Mt. 7:7; 19:12).[9]

Establish policies before a crisis. A vital part flowing from

---

6 Jack Dominian, *Marriage, Faith, and Love* (London: Darton, Longman and Todd, 1981), 224.
7 Harold Ivan Smith, "Life Beyond the Aisle," *United Evangelical Action*, 39 (Fall 1980), 18.
8 Smith, 18.
9 Andrew Cornes, *Divorce and Remarriage: Biblical Principles and Pastoral Practice* (Grand Rapids: Eerdmans, 1993), 325.

preventative techniques is to have policies in place on marriage, divorce, and remarriage before any crises occur. Unfortunately, churches often have no official policy regarding divorce and remarriage. Most lay people seem to feel that such concerns are the sole responsibility of the pastor. Consequently, persons facing these issues are thrown into a limbo of doubt and indecision. The pastor who leads a congregation may have a different standard from the previous one. Only when a crisis comes to a marriage do those involved discover what that standard is.

But the church, not just the pastor, does play a vital role in these matters. It is the cultural context in which both pastor and members operate. It needs a clear policy for dealing with divorce and remarriage, for it has not always effectively played its role.

Because of the pastor's position as leader of the church, it falls upon pastors to ensure that the church has a clear-cut policy in regard to divorce and remarriage. They may facilitate the creation of such a policy by teaching the congregation what the Bible says and what theological implications arise as a result. They should invite and animate interaction with their people.

There are doubtless dangers inherent in such a move. Care must be taken that any policy is set neither too broad nor too narrow. It must be based on Christian love and not on law. It must be dynamic and flexible, not rigid. Following the enactment of such a policy, church leaders must ensure that the people are informed as to what it is. They can do so through the church's various ministries of teaching, preaching, and counselling. And they must do so repeatedly.

Recognition of human failure. The church must recognize that human beings fail in the marriage endeavour just as they fail in every other aspect of human existence. It is a strange rationale that permits the church to accept former drug-addicts, thieves, murderers, child-molesters, and rapists, but refuse to acknowledge and receive those who are formerly married.

In recognizing human failure in marriage, the first task of the church is forgiveness. Integral to forgiveness is acceptance. It is not necessary to gloss over the fact that sin is always back of divorce; but it is to say with Jesus, "Neither do I condemn you. Go and sin no more" (Jn. 8:11). Wayne Oates has suggested that one reason the church finds its difficult to forgive the divorced is because it realizes that it is partially responsible for their dilemma: "We should not reduce the weight of sin, condemnation, and guilt attached to divorce. Rather, we should distribute it and accept our fair share of it."[10]

Another essential part of accepting failure and extending forgiveness is facilitating healing. Divorce is not unlike death in that both involve a loss of spouse, change of status, changed economic circumstances, and abrupt sexual deprivation. In some respects, divorce may be even more traumatic than death, for the person suffering marriage breakdown usually has had to contend for months with feelings of bitterness, hostility, loneliness, and fear.[11] What is more, while divorce may settle a major problem in marriage, many of the emotional and spiritual issues which caused it may linger on for years.[12] The church must make itself a healing community in which the needs of the divorced person, emotional, psychological, spiritual, financial, can begin to be met.

A vital element in the healing process is reconciliation. It is tragic that some churches will talk about allowing divorced persons to be fully restored to their fellowship and then will refuse them full and complete membership in practice. Frequently, divorced persons are allowed to be members, but they are excluded from holding positions as elders or deacons. It is sad when the church will allow offices to be held by members whose marriages have, in fact, long ceased to be biblical, "one-flesh" unions, but are still legally contracted, and will refuse such offices to those who have at least been honest enough to admit that they have failed. Until a church can accept forgiven divorced persons on the same basis as every other forgiven sinner, no true reconciliation has taken place. As someone has noted, "Retribution is God's concern, not ours. Restoration, renewal and concern are our responsibilities."[13]

Towards marriage. The scriptural exegesis on the divorce and remarriage passages pointed to the assumption that remarriage would frequently follow a divorce. Part of the church's obligation in the reconciliation and restoration of persons whose marriages have failed is to support and affirm them in that period following divorce, and to prepare them for life either as a single person or a remarried one.

One task incumbent upon the church is the exercise of discipline. Divorce usually means the abrupt cessation of sexual intimacy.

---

10 Wayne E. Oates, *Pastoral Counseling in Social Problems: Extremism, Race, Sex, Divorce* (Philadelphia: Westminster Press, 1966), 108—09.
11 G. Edwin Bontrager, *Divorce and the Faithful Church* (Scottdale, PA: Herald Press, 1978), 166—67.
12 Bernard Ramm, *The Right, the Good, and the Happy* (Waco, TX: Word Books, 1971), 90.
13 Arthur Gay, "Restoring the Divorced Christian," *United Evangelical Action*, 37 (Winter 1978), 17.

Studies have shown that a great many divorced persons have a problem coping without sex. While the church may sympathize with such a difficulty, it cannot condone promiscuity. Thus, it must be prepared to counsel the divorced person in the maintenance of celibacy and, if self-discipline wanes, to exercise discipline on behalf of the community.

It is important to emphasize once more that every single person — whether never married, or widowed, or divorced — should ask if marriage (or remarriage) is God's calling for him/her. Some people have been given a gift of celibacy and should exercise it better to serve God. Others must heed Paul's counsel that marriage is preferable to the unquenchable passion that may lead to promiscuity (1 Cor. 7:9). It is the church's responsibility to help all these people in general, and divorced persons in particular, to work through God's will in this matter.

Where remarriage is indicated, the church can facilitate it as a part of the reconciliation process, thus demonstrating that God's grace can conquer the opinion that remarriage following divorce is adulterous, and replacing it with the trust that whatever sin caused the demise of the first marriage, God's grace will be sufficient to sustain this new union.[14] Only in the context of the Christian faith, in fact, can remarriage following divorce become theologically justifiable and practical. Only within the love and affirmation of a congregational community can two people who desire to forge a successful union discover that possibility.[15]

The church's obligation, then, is two-fold. It must proclaim loudly and clearly that God's will for human beings in marriage is a lifelong union of one particular man and one particular woman who have jointly heard his call. At the same time, realizing human weakness and fallibility, it must help divorced people to put their failures behind them and build a second union that will endure and so glorify God. This it does by becoming a healing community with a listening heart and helping hands.[16]

To carry out such a mission will not be easy. As one concerned Christian counselor has put it:

> We cannot be content with sitting in ivory towers or standing behind insulated pulpits propounding the meaning of Bible verses on divorce and remarriage, turning them into precise laws that shut people out of our churches. Doing so assumes a moral, legal, and

---

14 Kysar, 104.
15 Bontrager, 176.
16 Margaret J. Rinck, "Becoming a Healing Community," *Christianity Today*, 36 (14 December 1992), 36.

cultural analysis that no longer exists... We must become deeply involved with those whose marriages have failed: the separated, the divorced, those contemplating remarriage, and married couples with struggling "blended" families. Without compromising scriptural standards, we must take the risk of asking the ultimate missionary question: How can we work with broken people and shattered marriages *in this particular setting?*[17]

Implications for the Divorced

While the church may occasionally fail to accept the divorced and minister to them, no one is as hard on the latter as they are on themselves. It is not infrequent for the divorced person to feel the oppression of debilitating guilt. There are, however, certain theological implications arising from a study of the Scriptures that may serve to bring release.

Divorce may be a morally valid decision. Both before and after a divorce, the Christian may suffer from the conviction that for believers divorce is always wrong. Such a person is then caught between the tensions of an unfulfilling, intolerable marital situation and a seemingly absolute biblical prohibition on divorce. But just as Jesus proclaimed that "the Sabbath is made for man, not man for the Sabbath" (Mk. 2:27), may it not be said that marriage was made for man and not man for marriage? If the institution of marriage is doing violence to the person, then it follows that the institution must be amended to allow the person to flourish.[18]

A marriage can die. Even Jesus recognized this fact. He did not care for divorce, but he was realistic in recognizing that Moses had allowed for divorce because of human hard-heartedness. Moses' law was a means of keeping the sin from being compounded.[19] Sexual infidelity, desertion, spiritual separation, and cruelty are all ways of dealing marriage a death blow. Divorce is often an honest way of admitting that a marriage is dead.

It is not unusual for a marriage to die and the spouses to continue to live together for years, stoically enduring the agony of spiritual and emotional separation (and often, of physical separation, as well), while giving little indication to the outside world that their one-flesh union has long since ceased to exist. To commend such a state of

---

17 David Seamands, "A Marriage Counterculture," *Christianity Today*, 14 December 1992, as viewed on website www.christianitytoday.com/ct/2000/135/44.0.html.
18 Robert F. Sinks, "A Theology of Divorce," *Christian Century*, 94 (April 20, 1977), 278.
19 James G. Emerson, "Marriage and Remarriage: Questions About Forgiveness," *Sex, Family and Society in Theological Focus*, ed. John C. Wynn (New York: Association Press, 1966), 149—50.

affairs over and above the honesty of divorce is to add to a tragic failure the sin of hypocrisy.

Divorce may therefore be a morally valid decision in which God's purposes are better served than by continuing under the marriage covenant. If one has done everything in one's power to make the marriage succeed and, in spite of such efforts, it has disintegrated, then divorce is undoubtedly the most moral alternative. It is better to be divorced than to be destroyed emotionally, spiritually, and perhaps, even physically.

Divorce is not unforgivable. Some divorces are out and out acts of sin in which one of the spouses is clearly the guilty — or, guiltier — party. The partner who commits sexual infidelity and then deserts his/her mate, for example, is without question guilty of horrendous sin.

At the same time, one who has been guilty of such offence and who comes to his/her senses, must be helped to realize that, although the marriage has been destroyed, all is not lost. Forgiveness and renewal are available in and through Jesus Christ.

In his First Epistle to the Corinthians 6:9ff., Paul points out that "unrighteous ones will not inherit the kingdom of God... neither the sexually perverse, ...not adulterers, ...nor homosexuals..." But in verse 11 he notes, "And some of you were these things, but you were washed; you were sanctified; you were justified in the name of the Lord Jesus." It is clear, then, that divorce is hardly unforgivable. Even the worst sinner may find justification through Christ.

Redeeming marriage. Divorce has been defined as a falling short of God's ideal for man and woman in marriage. Its origin is always in sin. Nonetheless, God allows for divorce to prevent greater and more tragic sin. Remarriage following divorce, therefore, is a similar deviation from God's ideal. While it may be seen as a fresh start for the divorced person, a new opportunity to establish a one-flesh commitment, one must realize that it arises out of colossal failure.[20] If that failure is not to recur, certain preventive measures must be taken.

While mention is made of the "guilty" party and the "offended" party, it is often impossible in a divorce to speak realistically in terms of innocence or guilt. When a marriage fails, usually both parties are guilty (at least, to some degree).[21] Guilt extends beyond the couple: Society, the children, the church are all guilty. That we are all

---

20 Stanley R. Ellisen, *Divorce and Remarriage in the Church*, rev. ed. (Grand Rapids: Zondervan, 1980), 73.
21 Though it is acknowledged that one party may be (considerably) more guilty than the other.

involved interpersonally necessitates that we all share the guilt for marriage breakdown.[22]

If the divorced person is going to avoid bringing the baggage of hurtful experiences from the old marriage into the new, he/she will have to repent of his/her own part in the activities and attitudes which led or contributed to the divorce. While the erosion of love can fracture the one-flesh union and legalities may civilly end the marriage, without repentance two spouses are still bound together by chains of guilt.[23]

Along with repentance, the divorced person must seek to be reconciled before God to his/her previous partner. To seek such a reconciliation does not necessarily mean to seek to be reunited to that partner in matrimony. Indeed, it may be better not to be. Many marriages that fail should never have been undertaken at all. But the former partners may be reconciled in spirit, each forgiving the other and finding peace with God as well. Even if the former spouse refuses to be reconciled, the very fact of the attempt and of unilateral forgiveness by the other will bring the forgiving partner liberation and peace. Until such a process has been worked through, a formerly-married person is unprepared emotionally and spiritually to embark upon another relationship. Second marriages tend to fail because of the failure of a formerly-married spouse to let go of the destructive aspects of the first marriage.[24]

It is of equal importance to the success of a new marriage that the divorced Christian marry only a believer. Any marriage has stresses and strains, but especially second marriages. There is no need to add the onerous burden of a spouse who cannot be sympathetic to nor share the spiritual ideals of his/her intended. Deliberately to marry an unbeliever is to deny the redemptiveness of the marriage and to deprive the union of God's blessing.[25]

Implications for Pastoral Leadership

Many of a church's attitudes are determined by its leadership, particularly by its pastoral leadership. It has been said that, as the pastor goes, so goes the church. How the pastor treats divorce and remarriage will crucially affect the official view of the church.

The pastor as facilitator. Pastors must facilitate the church's carrying out of its mission of transmitting the love and mercy of God. They must instill in the people a realization of God in Christ calling

---

22 Emerson, "Marriage and Remarriage," 152.
23 Bailey, 83.
24 Gay, 16.
25 Ellisen, 75.

everyone to come to Him, to have their needs met and their wounds healed, whatever their former state. Pastors must help the church in its mission to communicate to the world that Christ is adequate in every kind of situation, including divorce and remarriage.[26]

It is probable that those pastors who teach in such a fashion will encounter opposition. There are church members who believe that divorce and remarriage rank as the worst sins imaginable. They believe that if a church is open and forgiving to divorced persons, it is encouraging the breakdown of marriage.[27] Of course, to take such a concept to its logical conclusion would mean that no sin could be forgiven, whether gossip, theft, jealousy, etc., for fear of encouraging more of it. The church's attitude should be that of Paul Tournier:

> I cannot approve of his (the divorced person's) course of action, because divorce is always disobedience to God. ...But I know that this disobedience is no worse than the slander, the lie, the gesture of pride of which I am guilty every day. The circumstances of our lives are different, but the reality of our hearts is the same.[28]

If members of the congregation can be led to put themselves in the place of the divorced one, they will be much further down the road to mediating God's compassion and forgiveness.

The pastor and the restoration of the divorced. In any of the pastor's efforts to facilitate the mission of the church, none is more important than his/her own personal attitudes. Pastors must never forget that they are considered by most church members to be models for appropriate Christian behaviour. No exception is made in their ministry to those who suffer marriage breakdown. They must mediate forgiveness to them in the spirit of Christ, seeking their restoration.

Part of the process is to help divorced people in facing up to their guilt and in repenting of their hard-heartedness. But when pastors do so, they must take care to avoid certain errors. They must avoid implying that divorce (or remarriage) is a greater sin than others and that therefore greater penitence is needed. They must also resist members of the congregation who would seek to inflict upon the penitents some greater penalty because of their sin.[29]

The most important part of the restoration of the divorced person is the facilitation of his/her inclusion into the church as a full member with all the rights and privileges pertaining thereto. The church is not perfect, and it is therefore inconsistent to withhold church

---

26 Bontrager, 136–37.
27 William L. Coleman, "The Minister's Workshop: Ministering to the Divorced," *Christianity Today*, 19 (June 20, 1975), 29.
28 Paul Tournier, *The Person Reborn*, trans. Edwin Hudson (New York: Harper and Row, 1966), 71.
29 Coleman, 30.

membership in any respect from such a one[30] (i.e. the repentant person should be as acceptable for the diaconate as the repentant drunkard, proud person, or spiteful person). The divorced person, therefore, should have the opportunity of using his/her gifts in ministry just as any other member. In fact, the divorced person is not likely to corrupt others by his doctrine or behaviour; it is more likely that the trauma he has undergone will help him (all things being equal) to be more concerned for others.[31]

The pastor and the remarriage of the divorced. One of the best ways for pastors to facilitate the congregation's acceptance and affirmation of divorced persons is their willingness to participate in their remarriage. If one who has been divorced and who has worked things through decides on a new marriage, then the pastor should be open to performing that wedding.

A pastor's decision to perform any wedding is an important one. There is no suggestion here that clergy should be more permissive in the matter of the divorced person who remarries than of the never-before-married. In fact, just the opposite is true. If anything, a pastor should take even greater care to ensure that there is potential for the success of a second marriage.

Considerable counselling will be needed. Has the divorced person worked through his/her guilt from the last marriage to the point where it will not be destructive to a new marriage? If there are children, has thought been given to their reaction and potential adjustment to a new parent and authority figure in their home? Do the couple feel affirmed among this pastor's congregation? If not, they should seriously consider a different church home, one that will receive them in full and loving fellowship. All these questions and more need answering. Only when a pastor believes that the marriage will be an enduring, biblical union should it take place.

Furthermore, the pastor should have no qualms about the situation. A case is cited where the pastor was so bound up in uneasiness about the whole affair that he could not adequately minister to the couple. Such a one is like the minister with considerable experience who said, "I really don't know what to do; I just feel my way along. Sometimes I stand very rigidly by the rule and marry only the innocent party; other times, the two people seem so sincere that I cannot do otherwise but marry them."[32] Until a pastor can take a firm stand on an issue, based upon a clear perception of it, effective ministry to persons involved is extremely difficult, if not impossible.

---

30 Bontrager, 155.
31 Coleman, 30.
32 Emerson, *Divorce, the Church, and Remarriage*, 25—26.

Conclusions

The community of faith must have a theology of divorce and remarriage that adequately reflects both the will and the grace of God. If a church is a redemptive community, then it must hear the voice of the Lord commanding it to mediate his love and mercy to everyone. No one is to be excluded: not the divorced, nor the remarried, nor anyone else.

To extend the grace of God to the divorced does not require a retreat from the recognition and proclamation of lifelong, indissoluble marriage as God's ideal. One must realize, however, that there are degrees of success and failure in attempting to live up to that ideal (or to any of God's ideals, for that matter!). Thus, while holding to God's standard, the church must deal redemptively with those who fail to meet the standard and whose marriages fall apart.

The key words for all concerned are *repentance, forgiveness*, and *restoration*. The church must maintain an atmosphere which makes it easy for the divorced to seek repentance, to experience God's forgiveness in Christ, and to be accepted as full members of the community of faith. The divorced persons must be brought to the realization that these steps are necessary to their own spiritual, emotional, and physical wholeness. The pastor is to facilitate these things both within the church and among the divorced.

The rationale for remarriage derives from the reality of God's grace.[33] It is evidence of God's desire to do a new thing in the failed human life, to bring forth joy from sadness, success from failure. It is true that it is totally undeserved, but that is how God's grace always operates in the face of sin. It is indeed possible for a divorced person to enter a marriage which is so completely centred in the love and purpose of Christ that any divorce of that marriage will be impossible.[34]

The church, its leadership, and its members must be bold in standing for activities and attitudes that reflect God's grace. They must reject legalism as untenable and intolerable. God does not work on that basis, nor should they. The divorced may be reclaimed; remarriage may be redeemed, all to his glory.

---

33 Dwight Hervey Small, *The Right to Remarry* (Old Tappan, NJ: Fleming H. Revell, 1975), 183.
34 Small, 185.

Excursus

Clergy Divorce

The breakdown of marriage and the family has been one of the most serious problems of the church in this century. What is, if possible, even more alarming is the incidence of this problem among clergy. The percentage of clergy divorce is fast approaching that of the population as a whole.

If a divorced person proves an embarrassment to the church, how much more so a divorced minister! Even in churches that take an open and affirming stance towards divorced persons, the divorced minister is regarded with malaise, for clergy couples are expected to model marriage for their congregations.

Because of the position of the pastor as leader of the church, there are questions which need to be examined. In view of the Protestant belief that all believers are priests to God, should a minister be treated any differently from others in the congregation? Does divorce disqualify one from serving as a professional minister? Does it nullify God's call in this regard?

Attitudes Towards Clergy Divorce

The Old Testament gives evidence that leadership did make demands upon one's lifestyle which were different from those of ordinary Israelites. Moses was forbidden to enter the Promised Land because he failed to obey God's directions to the letter (Num. 20:12). Eli was rebuked by God and his posterity humiliated because he failed to control his sons (1 Sam. 2:27). Saul lost his throne because of disobedience (1 Sam. 13:8–15).

The New Testament holds similarly high standards for spiritual leaders. The Pastoral epistles (specifically, 1 Tim. 3:1–13; Titus 1:5–9) lay down qualifications for church leadership which are exemplary.

At the same time, there are situations in both testaments where a leader's sin was forgiven and he was allowed to continue to serve the Lord. In spite of David's adultery-murder (2 Sam. 11:1–12:15), he continued to reign over Israel. Peter denied his Lord three times (Mk. 14:66–72), but he became one of the premier leaders of the church. Biblically, a hard and fast rule is impossible by illustration.

In modern times, there is a similar dichotomy of opinion on the treatment of divorced clergy. One group advocates the expulsion of divorced persons from their positions, citing 1 Timothy 3:1ff.: "The implication was that there *were* members of the church who did *not* have those characteristics. *But* they should *not* be leaders."[1] Helmut Thielicke stresses that, while the minister possesses no special place within the universal priesthood, he is nonetheless subject to special demand on the ground that his message and particularly his performance of weddings would become suspect if his own marriage had failed.[2] Even if he is the "innocent" party, "it is obvious that the minister must give up his office or should be urged to do so."[3] Thielicke is more worried about the credibility of the office than about the office-bearer.

But there are those who believe that the same mercy and grace which are shown to divorced lay persons should also be shown to divorced clergy. If a divorced person seeks ordination and can show possession of "the important personal, interpersonal, and transpersonal characteristics for ordination," then the church should be open to it.[4] If a pastor in service enters into divorce proceedings, then the church has an obligation in Christian love to dialogue with that individual in an effort to determine whether continued service would be helpful or hurtful.[5] One divorced minister's wife voices the opinion of many when she asks, "why should the clergy be placed in a more legalistic category with regard to the scripture (than the laity)? A double standard is hypocritical and unwarranted."[6]

The Husband of One Wife

Because many arguments against allowing divorced persons to serve as ministers are based on 1Timothy 3:3, a closer look at the passage is desirable. Is the writer forbidding divorce and remarriage? The Greek words literally are "a one woman man" or "a one wife man". Whether the term refers to one at a time or one for a lifetime is in dispute.

There are at least five meanings that one may assign to this term. First, the writer may refer to the necessity for an overseer (minister) to be married. Secondly, the meaning may be that the candidate not

---

1 James Berkebile, "Here I Stand," *Brethren Life and Thought*, 21 (Summer 1976), 163. Italics his.
2 Helmut Thielicke, *Theological Ethics*, trans. John W. Doberstein (Grand Rapids: Eerdmans, 1964), 3.176.
3 Thielicke, 177.
4 G. Wade Rowatt, "Divorced: An Open Perspective for the Church," *Review and Expositor*, 74 (Winter 1977), 60.
5 Rowatt, 60.
6 Ernestine Hoff Emrick, "I Chose Honesty," *Brethren Life and Thought*, 21 (Summer 1976), 141.

be a polygamist. Or, he must be faithful to his wife, not possessing a concubine or a mistress. Fourthly, he must not be divorced and remarried. Lastly, he must not be a widower who has remarried.[7]

It is easy to reject the first possibility. It is unlikely that Paul would enact a qualification that he himself could not meet. Nor is the last possibility difficult to exclude. When one considers what Paul taught about death totally dissolving a marriage, and about the freedom to remarry in such an event (Rom. 7:1–3), it is unimaginable that he would then forbid a remarried widower to hold pastoral office.

One might see the second possibility as the centre of Paul's focus. Polygamy was common in New Testament times. Some have argued that it was not permitted in the early church. But what of those polygamists who were converted to Christianity? To desert their wives would have been completely against the spirit of Christ's teachings. To refrain from conjugal activity would have been to beckon promiscuity. In such a world where it was not uncommon for a man to have a multitude of wives (a condition which contradicts God's will for a one-flesh union), one should not be surprised at the restriction to a single spouse.[8]

Nor is the third option impossible to envision. The prospective pastor must be completely faithful to his wife. Sexually perverse activities abounded in the culture from which most of these converts had come:

> There was the regular institution of the *hierodoulai*, pagan temple prostitutes; the common custom of having *hetaerae* ("companions"), girls from non-citizen families who were used by unmarried and married men; …Converts to the Gospel did not at once step into perfect sexual purity. Hence this proviso regarding the "overseer:" to begin with, a man who is not strictly faithful to his wife is debarred.[9]

Does Paul have divorce in mind here? It is highly improbable. Divorce always dissolves a marriage. It is true that divorce followed by remarriage may be adulterous, but nowhere in the Bible does one find any suggestion that a divorced person who has remarried is still considered the spouse of the first husband/wife. In fact, Deuteronomy 24:1–4 stipulates just the opposite, and Paul talks in 1

---

7 Ralph Earle, "1 Timothy," *The Expositor's Bible Commentary* (Grand Rapids: Zondervan, 1978), XI, 366.
8 See William Barclay, *The Letters to Timothy, Titus and Philemon*, *The Daily Study Bible*, 2nd ed. (Edinburgh: Saint Andrew Press, 1960), 87–90 for detailed examples of such a situation.
9 R.C.H. Lenski, *The Interpretation of St. Paul's Epistles to the Colossians, to the Thessalonians, to Timothy, to Titus, and to Philemon* (Columbus, OH: Wartburg Press, 1937), 579.

Corinthians 7:11 of a divorced woman being unmarried. Furthermore, the charge of adultery would have no bearing here any more than would a charge of former drunkenness in 1 Timothy 3:8 for deacons. When one repents of sin, it is blotted out (Isa. 44:22,23). This "husband of one wife" requirement does not necessitate the total absence of sin against the marriage relationship, but rather a demonstration that God's grace has been so much at work in the life of the ordinand that — should there have been any sin in these areas — such sins have been forgiven after genuine repentance and the new life in the power of the Holy Spirit is now in control.[10]

One interpretation of this expression is suggested by Ronald Ward in the light of Ephesians 5:25-33. The writer, he declares, was thinking of a person at the time of candidature for the position: Did his marriage function so as to fulfil the ideal? If so, then he and his wife were one. He was, in fact and in attitude and in spirit the husband of one wife. "Second marriage is not contemplated and rejected; it does not come into the picture at all."[11] Perhaps at one time he was among those of whom Paul remarked, "And some of you were these things" (1 Cor. 6:11), but no longer. It must be remembered that he was not a recent convert (1 Tim. 3:6). Consequently, he could not be disqualified on the ground of his marriage (first or subsequent) which was not recent in any event (1 Tim. 3:4; cf. Titus 1:6).[12]

Divorce and Call

Does the act of divorce nullify the call of God to perform the tasks of the ministry? To answer in the affirmative is to exalt the office of ministry above the other aspects of the work in which all the saints participate. Even worse, it exalts the person in the office above the other saints, for it suggests that he who fills the office must be better in every way. He must be incapable of human failing. He cannot be a party to weakness.

To answer in the affirmative is to make a legal divorce contract the standard of failure. It does not matter if one perpetuates a lie by putting up with a marital relationship that has lacked mutuality and respect for years. It is saying that one may be a pastor with a dead marriage providing that that marriage has not been officially

---

[10] Robert L. Saucy, "The Husband of One Wife," *Bibliotheca Sacra*, 131 (July 1974), 240.

[11] Ronald A. Ward, *Commentary on I and II Timothy and Titus* (Waco, TX: Word Books, 1974), 55.

[12] Ward, 55. Cf. Sydney Page, "Marital Expectations of Church Leaders in the Pastoral Epistles," *Journal for the Study of the New Testament*, 50 (1993), 105-120.

pronounced dead.

To answer in the affirmative is to declare that divorce is the greatest sin, for there are few others that would seem to necessitate such a step. A pastor could be envious and be forgiven, or bitter and be forgiven. Churches are willing to ordain former drunkards and repentant thieves. To refuse to accept those formerly married is to make divorce an unforgivable sin.

In fact, ministers are only people who are a part of the fellowship of believers. They are subject to the same failings and sins as the rest of the body. But they are also subject to the same divine grace and love which are given to all who repent.

Indeed, the experience of divorce, like any other experience, may help a minister to fulfill the calling of God more effectively in certain situations. It may help him to be more understanding of others, more ready to listen, quicker to affirm because the counsellor has walked in the same path as the counsellee. The pastor who has undergone a divorce may be better able to guide others with marital problems to experience God's love and direction in their own situation.

If a minister has been truly called by God, the call will not be nullified by divorce if there has been a repentant spirit. A person who has been divorced may still be called and used in God's service. Divorce may make answering God's call more difficult, but when God truly calls, he will also provide the means to respond.

As far as service in a particular church is concerned, each individual case must be examined on its merits. It may be that a pastor will need time away from the duties of a pastorate in order to facilitate the healing process after a divorce. It may be that too many people in the congregation will manifest wrong and sinful attitudes towards the divorce for that minister to remain in that fellowship. Hard-heartedness can destroy relationships other than marital. It may also be that the loving affirmation and call of the congregation to continue in active service will speed the renewal process. There certainly is no clear biblical warrant for denying ministerial office to a person solely on the ground of a divorce.

Select Name And Subject Index

A

Abandonment . . . . See *desertion*
Abbott, T.K. 33
Abbott, Walter M. 22
Abortion 26
Abuse 76
Adams, Jay E. 35, 40, 52, 66, 71
Adultery 7, 8, 9, 10, 11, 12, 13, 16, 17, 18, 19, 20, 21, 22, 23, 24, 25, 26, 27, 28, 40, 41*n*., 42, 51, 53, 58, 59, 68, 71, 73, 77, 78, 88, 93, 96
Albright, W.F. 57
Allen, Willoughby C. 57, 60
Allô, E–B 63
American Baptist Churches 25
Amram, David W. 56
Anglican Church of Canada 26
Anglicanism 15, 18–19, 20, 26
Annulment 21, 27, 42
Aquinas, Thomas 9
Arendzen, J.P. 7, 8
Arles, Council of 8, 20
Athenagoras 7
Atkinson, David 18
Augustine (of Hippo) 9, 11, 20

B

Bailey, Derrick Sherwin 72, 81, 89
Bainton, Roland 12
Barclay, William 95
Barre, Michael L. 33
Barrett, C.K. 31, 33, 62, 64, 66
Barth, Karl 37
Barth, Marcus 33, 34
Beare, Francis W. 60
Bennett, T. Miles 49
Berkebile, James 94
Blackwood, Andrew W. 46
Bland, Thomas A. 35
Blomberg, Craig 31, 59, 69
Bondi, Richard 37, 38
Bontrager, G. Edwin 85, 86, 90, 91
Bowman, John 54
Bratcher, Robert G. 67

Bride-price (*mohar*) · 31, 41
Bright, John · 45
Bromiley, Geoffrey · 24
Brown, Colin · 64
Bruce, F.F. · 33, 34
Brunner, Emil · 27, 78
Bucer, Martin · 15–16
Buckley, Theodore Alois · 11
Burkitt, F. Crawford · 56
Burrows, Millard · 41

C

Calvin, John · 12, 13, 16, 18, 23, 42
Canadian Baptist Ministries · 25
Cassuto, U. · 29
Catherine of Aragon · 15
Catholicism (Roman) · · · · · · 4, 9–12, 13, 14, 15, 16, 20, 21–23, 24, 25, 27
Celibacy · 12, 33, 60, 61, 63, 78, 86
Certificate (divorce) · 40, 46, 54, 57, 72
Chary, Théophane · 48, 50
Christenson, Larry · 74
Christian and Missionary Alliance · 24
Church · · · · · · · · · · · · · · · · · · 3, 4, 5, 8, 9, 10, 11, 14, 15, 19, 33
Church of the Nazarene · 25
Coiner, H.G. · 63, 67, 69
Cole, R.A. · 56
Coleman, William L. · 90, 91
Confession, Westminster · 17, 26
Conzelmann, Hans · 31, 62, 67
Cooper, Darrien · 74
Cornes, Andrew · 82
Councils, Little and Large · 14
Covenant, marriage · · · · · · · · · · · · · · · · · · · 31, 35–37, 52, 71, 77
Craigie, Peter C. · 40, 42
Cranmer, Thomas · 15
Cruelty · 11
Cullmann, Oscar · 62

D

Daube, David · 54, 57
Delitzsch, Franz · 30, 42, 48
Deluz, Gaston · 63
Dentan, Robert C. · 49, 50
Desertion · · · · · · · · · · · · · · · 13, 14, 18, 25, 27, 28, 74–75, 77, 79, 88
Dickinson, William C. · 16
Differences, irreconcilable · 75–76
Dissenters · 16–18

Select Name And Subject Index

Divorce Bill of 1857 · 18–19
Dods, Marcus · 31, 50
Dominian, Jack · 23, 82
Driver, S.R. · 40, 41
Duffield, G.E. · 15
Dungan, David L. · 63, 67
Dunn, James D.G. · 62
Dupont, Jacques · 51, 53, 54, 57

E

Earle, Ralph · 95
Edward VI · 16
Ehrlich, Rudolf J. · 34, 35
Elephantine · 36
Elvira, Council of · 8
Elliott, J.K. · 64
Ellisen, Stanley A. · · · · · · · · · · · · · · · · · · · 58, 72, 88, 89
Emerick, Ernestine Hoff · 94
Emerson, James G. · · · · · · · · · · · · · · · · · · · 25, 87, 89, 92
England, Harold Ray · 43, 49
Erasmus, Desiderius · 10, 11, 20
Essenes · 56, 57
Ewald, George R. · 52
Exception clause · · · · · · · · · · · · · · · · · · 52n, 56, 57–59, 68

F

Faithfulness · See *fidelity*
Fathers · 7, 9, 19, 20, 38
Fee, Gordon D. · 67
Feinberg, Charles L. · 45
Fidelity · 12, 37–38, 52, 72, 76
Filson, Floyd V. · 60
Fischer, James A. · 68, 69
Fitzmyer, Joseph A. · · · · · · · · · · · · · · · · · · · 53, 54, 58, 64
Forgiveness · 3, 77, 85, 88, 90, 92, 96
Fornication · 9, 18, 33 n, 34, 78
Francisco, Clyde T. · 42
Furnish, Victor Paul · 61, 66

G

Garland, David E. · 30, 78
Garland, Diana S. · 29–30
Gay, Arthur · 85, 89
God, image of · 29–30
Godet, Frederic L. · 66
Gordis, Robert · 47

Gould, Ezra P. · 55
Guhrt, J. · 36
Gundry, Robert H. · 54, 57, 58

H

Hardheartedness (human) · · · · · · · · · · · · · · · 54–55, 63, 76, 90
Harrell, Pat Edwin · 7, 8
Harrington, Nolan Patrick · 9
Harris, M.J. · 64
Hauck, Friedrich · 52, 59
Henry VIII · 15
Hermas · 7
Hertel, James R. · 23
Hillel, School of · 56, 57, 62
Hobbs, T.R. · 40, 45
Honeycutt, Roy L., Jr. · 45
Hudson, R. Lofton · 68
Hyatt, James P. · 46

I

Incest · 42, 43, 59, 71
Instone-Brewer, David · 58
Intercourse, sexual · · · · · · · · · 9, 16, 32, 34, 35, 37 n, 42, 52, 59, 66, 71, 85
Infidelity · See *Unfaithfulness*
Isaksson, Abel · 45, 57, 58

J

Jerome · 9
Jewett, Paul · 29
Jones, David C. · 50, 59
Jones, Douglas R. · 48, 49, 50

K

Kaysar, Myrna and Robert · · · · · · · · · · · · · · · · · · · 81, 86
Keener, Craig · 79
Kehl, Robert · 76
Keil, C.F. · 30, 42, 48
Kelly, Page H. · 48, 49
Kingsbury, Jack Dean · 50, 57
Knox, John · 16

L

Laney, Carl E. · 65, 67, 95
Law, Mosaic · 12, 15, 19, 39–45, 54
Lenski, R.C.H. · 55, 66

Leeuwen, Mary Stewart van 81
Lieber, David L. 39
Lisowsky, Gerhard 44
Luther, Martin 12, 13, 18, 74

M

Mace, David R. 41
Mackin, Theodore 26
Mahoney, Aidan 58
Malina, Bruce 59
Mann, C.S. 57
Marriage 3, 7
Marshall, I. Howard 51, 53
Maurice, F.D. 19
Mayes, A.D.H. 40, 43
McDonald, Beth Glazier 48
McFayden, John E. 66
McKane, William 31
Melancthon, Philip 15
Metzger, Bruce 54
Milligan, George 64
Milton, John 17–18, 20
Mitton, C. Leslie 34
Moffat, James 34
Moody, Dale 51
More, Thomas 10, 20
Morgan, Mirabel 74
Morris, Leon 50
Moulton, James H. 64
Mueller, James R. 56
Murphy, Francis X. 22
Murray, John 40

N

Neufeld, E. 31
Nichols, Charles 30–31
Noordtzij, A. 44
Neuner, Joseph 11

O

Oates, Wayne 84, 85
O'Connor, James Murphy 62, 63, 64, 69
Olthuis, James H. 37
Omanson, Roger L. 62
Origen 8
Orr, William F. 78

Osiander · 15
Ottosson, M. · 43

P

Page, Sydney · 96
Paget, Valerian · 10
Palmer, Paul F. · 36
Pastor(s) · 83, 84, 89–92, 97
Paterson, John · 47
"Pauline privilege" · 21, 27
Pedersen, Johannes · 44
Pedophilia · 71
Pentecostal Assemblies of Canada · · · · · · · · · · · · · · 24
Peters, George W. · 4, 77, 79
Pinnock, Clark H. · 4
Piper, Otto · 27
Plaut, W. Gunther · 30, 31
Plummer, Alfred · 31, 33, 65, 67
Polygamy · 18, 42, 49, 58, 95
Pope Leo XIII · 11
Pope Paul VI · 22
Pope Pius X · 11
Pornography · 71
Pospishil, Victor J. · 22–23
Presbyterian Church U.S.A. · 26
Prophets · 45–50
Protestantism, "Strict" · · · · · · · · · · · · · · · · · · · 4, 23–225
Protestantism, "Broad" · 4, 25–27

Q

Quesnell, Quentin · 60
Qumran · See *Essenes*

R

Rad, Gerhard von · 30, 43
Ramm, Bernard · 21, 23, 27, 85
Rawlinson, A.E.J. · 55n
Reconciliation · · · · · · · · · · · · · 10, 13, 19, 26, 50, 63, 72, 73, 74, 86, 89
Reformers · 4, 12–16, 20
Reisser, H. · 71
Renaissance · 10
Repentance · · · · · · · · · · · · · · · 7, 10, 16, 72, 73, 79, 89, 90, 92, 96, 97
Richards, Larry · 77, 78
Richardson, Peter · 61
Rinck, Margaret J. · 86
Robertson, Archibald · · · · · · · · · · · · · · · · · · · 31, 33, 65, 67

Robertson, A.T. 56, 67
Roman Catholicism, dissenting 4, 22–23
Roman Catholicism, official 4, 21–22
Roop, Eugene F. 37
Ross, Heinrich 11
Rowatt, G. Wade 94
Ryan, Dermot 22
Ryrie, Charles 24

S

Saucy, Robert L. 96
Schillibeeckx, Edward 36
Schulz, F. 59
Schweizer, Eduard 56, 60, 61
Seamands, David 87
Separation, spiritual 73–74, 77, 79
Shammai, School of 56, 57, 62
Shaner, Donald W. 54, 55
Simon, Francis 22
Sinks, Robert F. 87
Small, Dwight Hervey 47, 68, 92
Smith, John M.P. 48, 49
Smith, Harold Ivan 78, 82
Songer, Harold S. 56
Southern Baptist Convention 25
Stagg, Frank 52
Stauffer, Ethelbert 37
Stein, Robert H. 25, 68
Stock, Augustine 58
Stott, John 25, 37, 58
Sugden, Edward H. 18
Swidler, Leonard 41

T

Tertullian 8
Thielicke, Helmut 34, 76, 94
Thompson, J.A. 45, 46
Tournier, Paul 90
Toy, Crawford H. 31
Trent, Council of 11, 20, 21
Troth .... See *fidelity*
Tudor, Mary 15
Tyndale, William 14–15

U, V

Unchastity .... 56, 57, 58, 60 *n*.

Unfaithfulness · · · 10, 12, 27, 38, 47, 50, 52, 58, 59, 68, 71–73, 75, 77, 79, 88
Union, unity · · · · · · · · · · · · · · · 9, 14, 25, 30, 32, 33, 35, 37, 58, 72, 73,
United Church of Canada · 26–27
United Methodist Church · 26
United Presbyterian Church of North America · · · · · · · · · · · · · · · 26
Vatican II · 22
Vawter, Bruce · 53, 59
Vugteveen, Stanley L. · 81

W

Walther, James A. · 78
Wambacq, B.N. · 52
Ward, James A. · 47
Ward, Ronald A. · 96
Wells, David F. · 4
Wenham, Gordon · 24, 42, 44, 58
Wesley, John · 18
White, Ernest O. · 38
Wiebe, Phillip H. · 58
Winnett, Arthur Robert · 15, 19, 21
Wordsworth, Christopher · 18–19

X, Y, Z

Yamauchi, Edwin M. · 36
Yaron, R, · 42
Zoghby, Elias · 22

Index Of Scriptures

Genesis
1:26–28 · · · 29
1:27f. · · · 17
2:18 · · · 17
2:18–24 · · · 30
2:21–22 · · · 34
2:23 · · · 17, 34
2:24 · · · 17
21:9–14 · · · 43
21:11–13 · · · 44

Leviticus
2:7 · · · 44
2:14 · · · 44
7:7–14 · · · 39
18:25 · · · 43
25:23 · · · 43

Numbers
5:3 · · · 43
30:9 · · · 39

Deuteronomy
13:6ff. · · · 74
22:12–21 · · · 39
22:28–29 · · · 39
23:12–14 · · · 41
24:1–4 · · · 17, 39–43, 45, 95

1 Samuel
2:27 · · · 93
13:8–15 · · · 93

2 Samuel
11, 12 · · · 73
11:1–12:15 · · · 93

Proverbs
5:15–19 · · · 31

Isaiah
44:22 73
44:22–23 96

Jeremiah
3:1–8 . . . . 39, 45–47
16:18 43
31:31–34 37

Hosea
2 39
2:2–3 47
5:3 43

Malachi
2:10–16 47–50
2:14 31

Matthew
5:31f. 17, 50, 51–52
5:32 24
7:7 83
10:37 74
19:3–11 17
19:3–12 . . . . 50, 51, 53, 56–61
19:4–6 32
19:6 65
19:9 24
19:11 82
19:12 . . . . 68, 83
22:39 76

Mark
2:27 87
10:1–12 . . . . 50, 51, 53–56
10:11–12 68
10:9 65
14:66–72 93

Luke
16:18 . . . . 50, 51, 52–53, 68
17:3 72

John

Index Of Scriptures

8:11 84

Acts
15:36ff. 75–76

Romans
5:20 73
7:1–3 95

1 Corinthians
1:11 63
6:9ff. 88
6:11 96
7 50
7:1–9 32–33
7:7–11 61–65
7:9 . . . . 78, 86
7:10–16 . . . . 17, 61
7:11 95
7:12–16 . . . . 65–67, 74
7:15 . . . . 24, 74
7:26–28 79
7:32–34 78
7:40 73

Ephesians
4:16 35
5:21–33 . . . . 33–34, 36
5:25–33 96

1 Timothy
3:1ff. 94
3:1–13 93
3:3 94
3:4 96
3:8 96

Titus
1:5–9 93
1:6 96

Hebrews
13:4 34

www.ingramcontent.com/pod-product-compliance
Lightning Source LLC
Chambersburg PA
CBHW070930160426
43193CB00011B/1646